D1015088

Therapy Dogs

These are the wonderful therapy dogs you will meet throughout this book. They will show you the work they do and why it makes them so special. They are (from left) Saint, a LabradorRetriever/ German Shepherd Dog mixed breed, adopted at nine months from the Oklahoma City Animal Shelter, Angel, a Miniature American Eskimo, adopted at eighteen months from the Oklahoma City Animal Shelter, and Star (Tacara's Scarla Soignes Star, CD), a Belgian Tervuren, adopted at seven months through her breeder Linda O'Hare Newsome. All three have been altered and have distinguished themselves in therapy work, giving new meaning to the name "Man's best friend."

Therapy Dogs

Training Your Dog to Reach Others

Kathy Diamond Davis

HOWELL
BOOK HOUSE

Copyright © 1992 by Kathy Diamond Davis

All rights reserved. No part of this book may be reproduced or transmitted in any form or by any means, electronic or mechanical, including photocopying, recording, or by any information storage and retrieval system, without permission in writing from the Publisher.

Macmillan General Reference
A Simon & Schuster Macmillan Company
1633 Broadway
New York, NY 10025

Library of Congress Cataloging-in-Publication Data

Davis, Kathy Diamond.
    Therapy dogs : training your dog to reach others / Kathy Diamond
Davis.
          p.   cm.
      ISBN 0-87605-776-8 : $22.95
      1. Dogs—Therapeutic use. I. Title.
    RM931.A65D38   1992
    615.8′51—dc20   91-39836
                                                                                      CIP

10   9   8   7   6   5

Printed in the United States of America

Acknowledgments

To my dogs, Saint, Angel and Star. Living with them has been a bit of heaven on earth.

To my husband, Bill, for support of every kind and for serving as the model handler for photographs.

To my friends, for encouragement and help that made this book better in every way.

To God, for everything.

All photos are the work of the author unless otherwise noted.

Careful reading of this book will inform the reader of the risks involved in therapy dog work and how to avoid them. Qualified handlers doing therapy dog visits with trained dogs rarely cause accidents that result in injury. However, dogs and people are individuals, and the author cannot be held responsible for the actions or omissions of others working with therapy dogs. As in every other dog activity, each owner/handler must assume responsibility.

Language purists will notice the use of the word "person" when referring to patients, clients, children, participants, residents and others served by facility therapy dog visits. Please note that the term "patient" is a red flag in many facilities and considered unacceptable when referring to the people cared for. The reasons for this could fill a separate book!

The best term to use, then, is "person," plural "people," in spite of the awkwardness in language this sometimes causes. Courtesy, however, comes before language purity—the purpose of language is to serve people, not the other way around!

I also regret the necessity of referring to a dog as "it" when the gender is unspecified. Be assured that I don't think of *any* dog as an "it."

Contents

Chapter 1: Benefits Therapy Dogs Provide

1.1.	Orientation to Reality	2
1.2.	Focal Point for Attention-Deficit Problems	2
1.3.	Morale	2
1.4.	Antidote to Depression	5
1.5.	Cooperation	5
1.6.	Social Stimulation	7
1.7.	Need for Touch	9
1.8.	Socialize Children to Dogs	11
1.9.	Working with Therapists	13
1.10.	Incentive	13
1.11.	Getting "Out of Yourself"	13
1.12.	Practicing Physical Skills	15
1.13.	Something to Look Forward to	15
1.14.	Emotional Support to Staff and Family	17

Chapter 2: What Kind of Dog?

2.1.	Training	19
2.2.	"Somebody's Baby"	20
2.3.	Benefits to the Dog	22
2.4.	Benefits to the Handler	22

2.5.	Benefits to the Community	27
2.6.	What If You Don't Have a Dog?	28
2.7.	Publicity	33
2.8.	The Indoor Dog	33
2.9.	Parasite Control	34
2.10.	The Veterinarian	36
2.11.	Is Therapy Dog Work for You?	39

Chapter 3: Visits as a Group

3.1.	Help Handlers Get Started	41
3.2.	Aggressive Dogs	44
3.3.	Standards, Uninterrupted Service to Facilities	47
3.4.	Insurance	48
3.5.	Working with Facility Staff	48
3.6.	Indoor or Outdoor Visits?	50
3.7.	Education, Entertainment or Therapy?	51
3.8.	Cooperation Among Groups	52
3.9.	Does This Group Make You Proud?	53

Chapter 4: Visits with One Dog

4.1.	Greater Responsibility	55
4.2.	Win Approval of a Group	57
4.3.	Working with the Staff	58
4.4.	Quieter, Less Disruption to Facility Routine	61
4.5.	Stronger Focus	61
4.6.	Limits	61
4.7.	Rooms Versus Meeting Areas	63
4.8.	Making Changes	65
4.9.	The Approach	66
4.10.	Working with Children	68
4.11.	First Visits Awkward	71
4.12.	The Leash	71

Chapter 5: Conditioning the Dog to Handling

5.1.	The Motivators: Food, Praise, Petting and Play	73
5.2.	Teaching the Dog to Remain Still	75
5.3.	Picking the Dog Up	79
5.4.	Playing Games with Your Dog	81
5.5.	Retrieving	82
5.6.	To Tug or Not to Tug?	90

5.7.	Inhibiting the Bite	92
5.8.	Teasing	96
5.9.	Physical Discipline	98
5.10.	A Cuddle a Day . . .	101

Chapter 6: Basic Control

6.1.	Finding Help	107
6.2.	Basic Principles	110
6.3.	Come	113
6.4.	Sit-Stay	118
6.5.	Down-Stay	123
6.6.	Heel	127
6.7.	Training Collars	130
6.8.	Stand for Petting	132
6.9.	Greeting	135

Chapter 7: Social Skills

7.1.	Be in Control: Never Endanger the Public	140
7.2.	Be in Control: Never Endanger the Dog	141
7.3.	All Types of People and Situations	143
7.4.	Learn to "Read" People	148
7.5.	Courtesy in Public	148
7.6.	Put People at Ease	151
7.7.	Training in Public	152

Chapter 8: Extra Control Work

8.1.	Signals	158
8.2.	Treats	167
8.3.	Greetings: Shake Hands, Kiss	169
8.4.	Walking Skills	171
8.5.	Positions in Place	171
8.6.	Front, Finish, Move, Back	173
8.7.	Language	175
8.8.	Does Your Therapy Dog Need a Hobby?	177
8.9.	Tricks	178

Chapter 9: The Handler's Job

9.1.	Attitude	182
9.2.	Be Ready to Say No	183
9.3.	Water	185
9.4.	What to Wear	187
9.5.	Times of Day	188
9.6.	Limits	190
9.7.	Attention on Dog, Potential Injuries	192
9.8.	Territorial Range, Positions	199
9.9.	Handler as Interpreter	208
9.10.	The Handler Is Responsible	209

The author with Saint, Angel and Star relaxing at home.   *William Carl Davis*

A therapy dog provides people with emotional benefits through social instincts and skills all normal dogs have.

1

Benefits Therapy Dogs Provide

THIS CHAPTER WILL GIVE HANDLERS, especially volunteers, an overview of how their dogs can help people. For more in-depth information, talk to facility staff. They understand the needs of the people they serve, and are familiar with the individuals. Volunteers who work their therapy dogs in facilities become part of that facility's team.

In general, therapy dogs provide people with emotional benefits through the use of the dogs' social instincts and social skills. Emotional benefits are difficult to measure, which means therapy dogs often help people without anyone knowing exactly how. Staff observations of the benefits to people, volunteer dedication to control and safety when working dogs in facilities, and the fact that volunteers have been happy to donate their services, have all made possible the great progress and acceptance of therapy dog work. Research in this field is ongoing, and those looking for scientific or medical data on therapy dog work can increasingly find it. This book will not attempt to provide that information.

1.1. ORIENTATION TO REALITY

People are attracted to the sight of a dog. Filmmakers use this device frequently—sometimes having a dog move across the screen for no other reason than to get you to look! If you walk with your dog, you have surely noticed how people are drawn to it. This helps illustrate how a therapy dog can have the power to bring disoriented people into the moment. Some Alzheimer's sufferers and other people whose minds wander benefit from being brought mentally into the here and now as often as possible. Institutional living can make it a habit for them not to focus on the present. The dog can give them both a focal point and a reason to try.

It can take a disoriented person some time to organize his or her thinking. The therapy dog handler may need to spend extra time with the person, or come back later in the visit.

1.2. FOCAL POINT FOR ATTENTION-DEFICIT PROBLEMS

The same focal effect provides a benefit to children and others with learning disabilities. Many learning problems include the inability to concentrate. Until a person can concentrate, he or she can't learn. Think of the ability to concentrate as being like a muscle. The more it's used, the stronger it gets. When the person focuses on the therapy dog longer than he or she can normally concentrate on any one thing, this "muscle" can become gradually stronger. In some cases, the dog can also be used to help teach a child's lessons. However, the element of novelty is probably a factor, so part-time use of the dog, rather than at every session, may be most effective.

1.3. MORALE

Keeping good morale in a facility can be difficult. When the dog comes, morale invariably improves. I remember a dramatic example of an outpatient program for adults with emotional problems. When the therapy dog group I was with arrived, people from the program were verbally picking at each other and making negative remarks. The change in the environment was electric by the end of the visit, with almost everyone behaving positively. And after they

The therapy dog provides a focal point for the concentration of the person the dog is with.

A visit from a therapy dog frequently brings about a dramatic boost in the morale of those the dog comes in contact with.

3

For many reasons life in a care facility can become depressing. A visit from a therapy dog breaks the daily routine and stimulates renewed interest in the dog and the wider world it represents.

By its attitude, a well-trained therapy dog can favorably influence the people living in a facility and the staff that looks after them.

get to know me, people in the facility perk up even when I come in on an errand, because they associate me with the dog. Also, staff members in facilities frequently mention that therapy dog visits improve the morale for the day. This benefit seems to apply to every type of facility where therapy dogs work.

1.4. ANTIDOTE TO DEPRESSION

Therapy dogs have often been said to help people overcome depression. Physical inactivity can bring on depression, as can losing your home and living in a facility where life is routine. When the dog comes in, suddenly the day isn't boring.

A therapy dog is also a powerful antidote to handler depression! The physical exercise of taking care of a dog and training it, the touch involved in giving your dog its regular conditioning to handling, the emotional sense of connection to your neighborhood when you circulate with the dog to develop and maintain social skills and the sure knowledge of the benefits you provide to your community by doing therapy dog visits will keep your spirits in excellent shape.

1.5. COOPERATION

One benefit that endears therapy dogs to facilities is increased cooperation between staff and the people they take care of. This happens partly because of improved morale and other factors. But one way you as a handler can facilitate it is through your manner when working the dog. If you lovingly elicit good behavior from your dog instead of demanding it, you remind the staff how to deal with people. You aren't teaching them, since they already know how to treat people, but you make it easier to remember on difficult days. At the same time, your cooperative dog sets an example that many people will follow, by cooperating with the staff.

We aren't drill sergeants with our therapy dogs. Instead, we're loving partners. The handler is in charge, but just as a staff member is sometimes in charge when working with a person, being in charge is also a position of service. A good therapy dog handler serves the dog as they work together to help people.

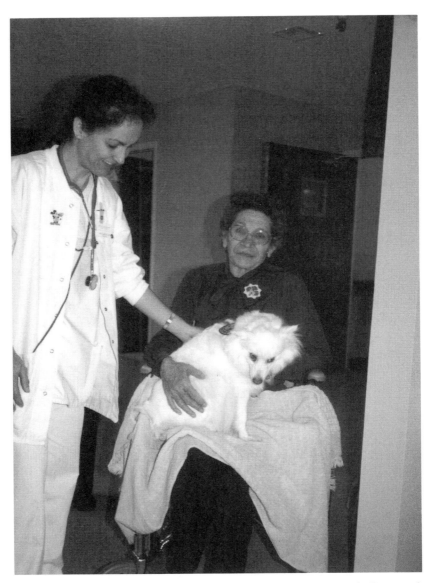

The social stimulation that a therapy dog triggers can get people in a facility out of their beds, dressed and interacting with others around them. Helping people forget about themselves and enjoy their world makes a therapy dog visit a potent catalyst.

1.6. SOCIAL STIMULATION

One reason therapy dog visits boost morale, alleviate depression and improve relationships among people is that they provide social stimulation. When you come in with the dog, people will talk to you, they'll talk to each other and they'll keep talking after you leave. If the facility is properly prepared for your visit, the talking will start before you come.

If you do your visits in meeting areas, social stimulation will be increased by getting people together and out of their rooms. This starts occuring more as people get to know the dog and begin coming out to see "their" dog. If they come out of their rooms, they may also get dressed and increase their physical activity, both positive behaviors. Staff members are always looking for ways to get people out of their rooms.

A mysterious and fascinating element adds to the ability of a dog to provide social stimulation. With three dogs in my house, I live constantly with dog language. I often hear and read about "animal ESP." I strongly believe that what people think of as extrasensory perception is normal sensory perception for dogs. If you spend enough time with your dog and have a close bond, the dog will manage to establish communication with you through its great skill with body language. Add the fact that dogs have physical senses far more acute than human senses, and it's not hard to understand how these seemingly extrasensory events occur. The most fantastic part is that dogs communicate very sophisticated information without speech.

When my three dogs chase a field mouse or other wild animal in the backyard, they're so focused that I make sure to interrupt them, never trusting that the stray animal will escape. You see, it's not a simple matter of the animal running faster than the dogs. My dogs live together as a pack, with well-established lines of communication and rank. Just as a pack of wolves would do when hunting for food, my dogs use intricate communication to tell each other "You go that way—I'll go this way," "Stop and hold your position," "Get around on the other side" and much, much more. They send and receive these messages with lightning speed—much faster than words. Anyone who lives with this long enough, with an open mind, will realize that much more than instinct is at work here. The dogs have to communicate and cooperate to accomplish such breathtaking chases. If it were a competition among them, they would seldom catch anything.

The need to touch a living being is very important to people living in a care facility. The therapy dog provides this wonderfully well, frequently awakening special memories fondly recalled.

Many people have experienced problems that have taken away their ability or desire to speak. When people stop talking for a while, it gets harder and harder to start again. It can get so hard that the person quits trying. Dogs are highly social animals. If you understand this about your therapy dog and provide it with the necessary opportunities to develop its social skills with humans, your dog will actually learn to communicate with people that other *people* can't communicate with. Somehow this communication from the dog can reach a person who has quit talking and help build a bridge back to speech. It can also help a child who's struggling against unusual difficulties in learning to speak for the first time.

One of the joys of handling a therapy dog is watching the dog communicate with other people. You can learn to read some of the signals but probably never all of them. It's a two-way conversation that never ceases to amaze me. This is perhaps the central reason to develop in your therapy dog the ability to work responsibly without tight control from you—i.e., the quality of initiative. Without it, you can't step back a pace and let your dog communicate on its own with another person. With it you can watch, absorbed, as this subtle ballet goes on between dog and human, understanding enough of it to assist your dog when needed. This same ability as a handler will give you time to react when a potential problem develops—if you're good at reading people and dogs, you'll almost always see trouble before it can happen. The more experience the handler has, the less risky this work becomes for the dog.

1.7. NEED FOR TOUCH

Another way that therapy dogs can help people is by meeting the universal need for physical touch. This need isn't satisfied by the neutral touching involved in physical care, although some special staff members give extra touch that fills this need, if they have time.

Some people living in facilities have healthy relationships with relatives or caring staff people to provide the necessary touch. Some don't. Many of us are uncomfortable hugging or otherwise touching strangers, or even people we know. Sexual taboos can also make it awkward for us to touch people. Whole books have been written on the subject of touch, which is an extremely important subject when dealing with therapy dogs. Not only must the dog be conditioned to

The therapy dog often represents an incentive for the person in a care facility to shake off the cobwebs of isolation and depression. Just the presence of the dog makes people want to touch and interact with it.

touch, but touch plays a major role in nonverbal communication between people and dogs. The handler needs to know—from lots of regular practice—how to read these exchanges and when and how to intervene.

1.8. SOCIALIZE CHILDREN TO DOGS

Another benefit therapy dogs can give is particularly relevant to working with children. Many children grow up without enough exposure to dogs to be able to relate to them in adulthood. Poor socialization of children to dogs, as well as poor education about dogs, leads to many dog-bite cases. These experiences can often be avoided or overcome by the use of a therapy dog.

I often tell busy parents who feel guilty about not having a dog that children learn far more from time with a trained therapy dog and handler than they would from having a dog at home that no one has time to take care of or train. With a therapy dog and handler, the child is never knocked down or bitten and the child learns the best of dog behavior. At the same time, the therapy dog gains additional experience with children—vital for handlers who don't have children of their own.

While education about dogs and gaining a positive image of dogs is important for people of any age, the most important period may be during childhood, up to the age of six. During the first five or six years of life, children learn new languages (including dog language) with ease, and develop lifelong social skills. If communicating with a dog is part of this time in their lives, it will be easier for children to communicate with dogs for the rest of their lives. This benefit is also important for any child with a disability who might be helped later in life by a trained service dog. He or she will need to be able to bond with a dog and communicate with it. This includes children who are blind, deaf or who must use wheelchairs. Those who use assistance dogs also benefit from therapy dogs and their handlers helping dogs to gain public acceptance.

Children are a special challenge for the therapy dog, but dogs and youngsters usually understand one another and communicate on a level not reached by all.

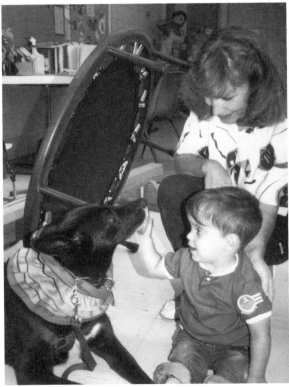

1.9. WORKING WITH THERAPISTS

Increasingly, therapy dog handlers are working directly with licensed therapists. In such cases, a professional works with the person toward specific therapeutic goals while the handler works with the therapy dog to assist in those goals. Working directly with a professional therapist is a special opportunity for you as a therapy dog handler, because in this case you get much more feedback than on other types of visits.

Generally, the therapy dog will be a special treat for the person being helped and will not come to every therapy session. Since therapists do sessions both with and without the dog, they can tell you how the dog helps. One thing they may tell you is that people are more relaxed in sessions when the dog is present. Instead of focusing on pain or frustration, people can focus on the dog. Having a dog in a therapy session can improve the person's morale and make him or her more willing to work at therapy exercises. Therapy can be a long and painful road. A dog is a great friend at such times.

1.10. INCENTIVE

A therapy dog can be used as incentive. The person being helped might be allowed to give the dog a treat or throw a toy for the dog to retrieve. Time with the dog, taking the dog for a walk or other interaction with the dog can be offered as incentive to get people to cooperate with staff, do their exercises, come out of their rooms or do other things that will benefit them.

1.11. GETTING "OUT OF YOURSELF"

The staff can increase benefits to people between therapy dog visits by using other activities in conjunction with the dog visits. People might draw pictures of dogs or have story-telling sessions to talk about their former pets. Groups might subscribe to dog publications or add dog books to the facility's library. People can watch the dog shows occasionally shown on cable television.

Most facilities do things to encourage volunteers—such as giving luncheons or certificates and writing thank-you notes, among other expressions of appreciation. People benefit therapeutically by

If you contemplate pursuing therapy dog work, arrange your schedule so that your visits occur at regular times. People in facilities come to look forward to the appearance of the therapy dog and disappointment in the dog's not appearing is not in the best interest of all concerned.

The emotional support therapy dogs provide to persons in facilities extends also to staff and family members, often making relations smoother all around.

being included in these expressions of thanks to the handler and dog. Besides benefiting the people, such things increase the therapy dog handler's commitment. Expensive gifts are not called for—if people want to give the handler and dog a gift, they should notice what is used on visits. A fresh can of tennis balls would delight many handlers. Avoid offering dog treats—people will want to see the dog eat them on the spot, which may not fit into the dog's diet or the handler's manner of working on visits.

Activities that give people a chance to think of someone other than themselves provide therapeutic benefits. When my dog Star was gravely ill, many of the people I visited with my other two therapy dogs prayed for her. As Star began to rally, and eventually made a dramatic and full recovery, we all rejoiced together. Thinking of and doing things for others alleviates depression and feelings of helplessness.

1.12. PRACTICING PHYSICAL SKILLS

A therapy dog can help people work on specific physical skills. Some people benefit greatly from learning to handle a trained dog on its commands. If you don't wish to have your dog obey commands given by others, you can do interactions that aren't commands. My dogs catch or retrieve soft toys people throw for them. Children can benefit in many ways from throwing a tennis ball for the dog.

People healing in a facility can walk a dog and benefit from the exercise, but beware of the risk of falls. The dog should be carefully matched to the person. I do not do this with my dogs.

Shaking hands is a cue rather than a command, so people can work on this and be rewarded when the dog responds. If you choose to let people give treats to your dog on visits, they can use treats to elicit trick responses from the dog that are not commands.

1.13. SOMETHING TO LOOK FORWARD TO

The benefit of something to look forward to depends on the handler's dedication to therapy dog work. The more consistent you are, the more the staff will count on you and pass the word that you will be there. It's amazing how long it takes for the routine of your

It is hard to know who needs the attention of a therapy dog when there is a visit to a facility. The concept is still new and constantly developing. In time we will probably find many more applications for the trained therapy dog and the implications are exciting for all concerned.

Courtesy Dog Fancy Magazine

visits to filter through to all the staff. You can make monthly visits for a year, and still have people who don't realize you come every month.

I find it useful to schedule visits for "the first Tuesday of every month," or similar designation, so that even though I confirm the date each time with the facility (setting the next date when I'm there each time), we both have something to plan around in advance. When a facility changes personnel, my visits are not interrupted. The fact that personnel does change, sometimes frequently, is another reason the stability of regular therapy dog visits benefits people.

I cancel, or preferably reschedule, a visit if I'm sick, the roads are icy, or a dog is sick and I have to stay with it. If I can safely leave a sick dog, I bring a different therapy dog. I seldom make changes, and the facilities have learned to count on me. When staff can confidently tell people the therapy dog is coming, visits provide the benefit of anticipation.

1.14. EMOTIONAL SUPPORT TO STAFF AND FAMILY

I often work with staff members or family members of people in facilities. This might not seem to be the job of a therapy dog and handler, but I'm convinced that sometimes it's vital. If you help a staff person, you help everyone that person takes care of. By helping someone's family member, you make it easier for that relative to continue to visit and care for the person who needs him or her. It's often a lot easier emotionally for a volunteer to visit than for a family member.

Therapy dog work is where you find it. We can't see into everyone's heart and read there who needs time with the therapy dog. I try to do my best with everyone. I'm sure we will be aware of even more ways for therapy dogs to help in the future. When people in a situation need emotional support, a dog and handler can probably be found who are suited to go there and give it. With training and a qualified handler, the dog is the best-suited animal to visit wherever there are people in need.

There is no right or wrong kind of dog to work in therapy. The determination of whether a dog has a chance of success hinges on the individual's temperament and receptiveness to training.

2

What Kind of Dog?

MANY THERAPY DOG GROUPS, local and national, set standards for their members. Criteria differ because the leaders have different ideas. In this chapter I will set forth some guidelines that are definite enough for all therapy dog handlers to understand, yet flexible enough to fit the many different kinds of therapy dog jobs.

2.1. TRAINING

Each handler decides on limits for his or her therapy dog work. In whatever facilities you choose to work, you must be able to control your dog at all times. That's a tall order, and I recommend control training for therapy dogs and their handlers. This training should teach both dog and handler the commands to Come, Sit-Stay, Down-Stay and Heel.

Therapy dogs work on leash most of the time, but training for off-leash control eliminates having to drag the dog around by the leash, or give severe neck jerks to maintain control—both taboo when working a therapy dog in public. And, on leash as well as off leash, training the dog to take the commands is of no use unless the handler is also trained to give commands and handle the dog properly. In addition, every dog is different, so handler and dog need to train together to become a team.

Control training on this level also gives handlers confidence and an understanding of their own and their dogs' limitations. Good training calms sassy dogs and nervous dogs alike while building a stronger bond between handler and dog. To bring a dog to this level of training takes perhaps six months. This would be quite soon to get a therapy dog ready, and the dog should be past puberty—at least a year old—before starting to work. A year to eighteen months is more realistic for most people to ready their dog, especially with the first dog. Some dogs need more time—even several years—to mature.

I won't say, though, that no dog should be allowed to serve as a therapy dog without this level of training. Training has many, many advantages, but dogs are serving well in some cases with little or no training.

As much as possible in therapy dog work, dogs and people should be included rather than excluded. An obedience instructor can often evaluate a dog and handler to determine if control is adequate. Facility staff members routinely make this decision. Some handlers without training have much natural ability, and so do some dogs.

2.2. "SOMEBODY'S BABY"

One special qualification of a therapy dog is what I'll call being "somebody's baby." If you haven't had experience with this work, you might think that a dog very attached to its owner wouldn't make a good therapy dog. The opposite is true. Just as a child needs loving parents (or someone early in life to give deep and unconditional love) to grow into an adult who can love others, a dog who will serve the public as a therapy dog needs loving support at home from at least one person that dog loves and trusts.

Interacting with friendly strangers is a job the dog learns to do, with the handler's help. A strong bond with the handler teaches the dog how to relate to a human, makes it possible for the dog to work under the handler's control, and gives the dog confidence. A strong bond also allows the handler to work the dog in a loving way that serves as a model for how others will treat the dog. When the handler relates to the dog with obvious love, everyone is assured that the

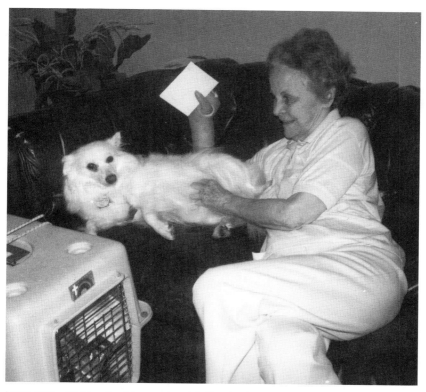

Interacting with friendly strangers is a job the dog learns to do with the handler's help. How well the dog learns is shown when it visits a facility.

dog is loved and well cared for. This greatly adds to the effectiveness of therapy dog visits.

2.3. BENEFITS TO THE DOG

Worldwide, dogs are divided into hundreds of different breeds and selectively bred for dramatically varied appearances and behaviors. Besides breed differences, dogs are individuals and vary from one another just as people do. Many dogs are working dogs that need jobs to do. With the right training, the same types of dogs that serve to guide the blind, assist people in wheelchairs and alert deaf people to important sounds also make excellent therapy dogs. Owners of well-adjusted working-type dogs know that such a dog isn't well adjusted without the responsibility and pride of a job of its own. Serving as a therapy dog can satisfy this need. It can mean the difference between a happy, well-behaved dog and a dog that shreds home furnishings or barks all day from frustration and boredom.

Many dogs aren't working dogs in this sense. They were bred to be pets, or for tasks like pest control that don't involve working under human direction. Some dogs won't enjoy therapy dog work, and certainly shouldn't be forced to do it. However, in most breeds there are at least a few highly sociable dogs who would be happier with extra people to love.

Many dogs enjoy going places, once they learn that nothing bad will happen when they get out. A therapy dog gets to go on visits and socialization outings. A therapy dog also gets more invitations when you go out with family and friends, because others know the dog will behave. The dog gets to spend more time with you because of its beautiful manners and enjoyment of other people. The dog has a more interesting life.

2.4. BENEFITS TO THE HANDLER

The benefits to the handler include all the benefits to the dog and more. If you enjoy being with your dog—and you do, or you wouldn't be interested in doing therapy dog visits—the extra opportunity to do things together is a big benefit. Some people satisfy their desire through dog shows and other events with the goal of earning titles on the dog. Unlike most such events, therapy dog work is a

Having a job to do is often the difference between a bored, frustrated animal and a happily fulfilled one. Therapy dog work provides this outlet and even has side benefits. Here Saint, always dependable, retrieves a misplaced cane in a large shoe store.

noncompetitive activity. People will compliment your well-trained and well-groomed dog, and thank you repeatedly for coming. Therapy dog visits do not require entry fees like dog shows do, and you may even be able to deduct mileage to and from therapy dog visits on your income tax as a charitable contribution. You may also have lower veterinary expenses than when showing dogs. Contaminated show grounds and dogs brought long distances expose dogs to disease, and shows are stressful. Therapy dogs can work close to home, around few other dogs, in clean conditions. Good handlers can make therapy dog work a low-stress activity for their dogs.

Dog shows are well established and likely to remain available to dog owners as a means of enjoying their dogs and learning more about them. Performance events help maintain and improve the abilities of working breeds. Many people find this is how they want to spend a major part of their lives with their dogs. These people will always be essential to therapy dog work, because dog shows are a major system for responsible dog breeding and training—and for the training of handlers.

Most people who take dogs through obedience classes don't go on to earn obedience titles in licensed trials. Many owners want well-behaved dogs but aren't interested in competition. Some of these people and their dogs are excellent candidates for therapy dog work. Other prospects for therapy dog work are the many people who participate in competitive events for several years before deciding to stop. I was one of these. I find therapy dog work more satisfying. The more dog show enthusiasts know about therapy dog work, the more therapy dog volunteers can come from this large number of well-educated dog people who, along with their trained dogs, find themselves "all dressed up and no place to go."

There are conflicts between therapy dog work and dog shows that force some dog owners to choose one or the other:

1. Therapy dogs should ideally be neutered. Conformation show dogs can't be shown—or bred—after being neutered.
2. Dog showing carries with it an obligation to support clubs and events, a serious time commitment. Therapy dog work also involves a serious time commitment, and there is only so much time!
3. The training for therapy dog work is different from either conformation training or obedience competition training. Some handlers and dogs will easily combine two or more

The priorities for a successful show dog and for a successful therapy dog are very far apart. If you show your dog and contemplate doing therapy work, it would be wisest to wait until the dog is no longer being shown or used for breeding before embarking on therapy work. What is required to make this Wire Fox Terrier a top show dog would work against the qualities we want in a therapy dog. *Cushman*

activities, but others will find that trying to do both can cause part or all of the work to suffer.

4. During show season, it may be impossible for serious exhibitors to keep up therapy dog visits. To do regular visits for part of the year until people get attached and staff gets into a routine, and then drop out during show season, is not the best way to serve the needs of therapy dog work.

5. The conformation show dog needs a correct coat. For some breeds, this calls for housing the dog outdoors and using a specialized grooming routine. The therapy dog needs to live indoors and be kept clean all the time—a lifestyle that can soften the coat, and result in a coat of the wrong texture and thickness for some breeds to win in the show ring.

6. Some competition training requires the dog to remain isolated except when working. The therapy dog needs as much contact with humans as possible, with a minimum of isolation.

7. In the conformation ring, the dog needs to stand like a beautiful statue when the judge approaches. A therapy dog needs to exhibit expressive body language when it meets people.

8. The competition obedience dog must respond to commands reflexively and without pausing to think to have a chance of winning. The therapy dog needs to think about each command and not respond reflexively. The instant response of the competition dog could be dangerous in a facility where there are hazards the handler may fail to see before giving a command. The dog must consistently hesitate and remain alert to the environment.

I'm not suggesting that people who show their dogs shouldn't work with therapy dogs. On the contrary, I think that clarifying these issues can help dog show enthusiasts participate in therapy dog work. Dog people are great problem solvers!

Those dog show enthusiasts who are not able to participate extensively in individual visits may be instrumental in educational and entertainment programs. They can also help recruit new therapy dog handlers by encouraging people who don't plan to show—or who retire from showing—to consider this work. They can place young, retired show dogs with experienced therapy dog handlers. They can work with handlers who don't own dogs, to train them to work retired show dogs that will continue living with their owners. This is a great way to make use of the show person's expertise, to train a new therapy dog handler and to give added meaning to the life of a retired show dog.

Obedience trial enthusiasts can promote classes to serve the pet-owning public as well as therapy dog handlers. Such classes need to differ from classes for competitive obedience. Dog clubs and private instructors who teach good therapy dog classes will find themselves much in demand, since this training suits the family dog as well.

I hope this book will serve obedience instructors wishing to learn about training therapy dogs. It is a different form of training than for any other job dogs do. One of the greatest benefits to the therapy dog handler is that this is a most enjoyable form of dog training. For those of us who find deep satisfaction in working with a dog as a partner, this is an excellent way to fulfill that desire.

2.5. BENEFITS TO THE COMMUNITY

Therapy dog handlers work regularly on social skills in public. Instead of being an intrusion, as when dogs are assisting disabled people (those dogs must ignore friendly people), the public helps train therapy dogs by petting them.

Handlers visit shops and other places with their dogs. They build a relationship with proprietors based on trust. In most communities, proprietors don't have to let therapy dogs in. It's up to the handler to earn this privilege. In the process, the public gains valuable insight into the proper way to care for and control a dog.

Area children benefit from having a therapy dog in the neighborhood. Working parents and city living combine to prevent many children from having a well-cared-for family dog with whom to grow up. When neighborhood children pet therapy dogs, handlers fulfill an important need for these families.

The neighborhood benefits from the handler educating other dog owners, resulting in fewer loose, neglected dogs. Therapy dogs and their owners show neighbors a standard of proper dog care and control to which they might not otherwise be exposed.

Therapy dog handlers are public relations representatives for responsible dog ownership. By example, we make it clear that if a dog is causing trouble in its neighborhood, something is wrong that can and should be corrected. In this role we help the community and help responsible dog owners, including dog show enthusiasts, to improve public acceptance of well-behaved, well-kept dogs.

2.6. WHAT IF YOU DON'T HAVE A DOG?

In this chapter you are probably expecting to learn how to select a therapy dog so you can get started. I'm sorry to say that it doesn't work that way. If you don't currently own a dog, or if your dog does not seem suited as a therapy dog, do not go out and get a dog as your starting point in this work. Your chances of success are so low that you'd probably have to find another home for that dog eventually.

Working with a therapy dog is a difficult handling skill, and requires excellent care of the dog at home. A beginner doesn't know how to do either, and in the process of learning you might well ruin the dog. It's all too easy to adopt a dog. Don't give in to the temptation to acquire a dog hastily, before you have properly prepared.

So how do you start? First, if you own a dog that you don't think is suited, seek skilled advice. You may need to change the way you care for and work with your dog at home and go through a training course with the dog. There may be nothing "wrong" with your dog.

Whether you own a dog or not, seek out local handlers who work with therapy dogs. This could include obedience trainers who do occasional visits. Go and watch some visits. If you still feel you want to do this, offer your services as a handler. You may receive valuable training with a trained dog. If and when the dog's owner feels you're ready, you may be able to take the dog on therapy dog visits, or the owner may bring it for you to handle while he or she works another dog. At some point you'll be ready to select a dog for yourself.

If owning a dog won't work for you, my experience indicates that there are many more dogs available for this work than there are handlers. You can probably do visits regularly without ever owning a dog. People, not dogs, are the shortage in therapy dog work.

If you are a therapist or an activities or social professional in a facility or in private practice, and are thinking about becoming a therapy dog handler, think twice. Would it be emotionally healthy for you to spend your free time volunteering in the same setting where you spend your working hours? Or, do you want to try to

The positive acceptance of therapy dog work gives rise to a wide variety of benefits. The young lady shown here, Michelle Dubites, did not own a dog when she began working with Candice, a retired conformation champion and obedience-titled Labrador Retriever, owned by Marilyn Smith. Like most breeders, Ms. Smith had other dogs needing her attention, so Candice and Michelle got busy on therapy work with Candice and her owner showing Michelle the "ropes." A volunteer was able to learn some valuable skills, a retired dog was able to get back into action and an involved friend of dogs performed a gratifying bit of matchmaking.

handle a dog and work with clients at the same time? Can you arrange for the dog to have some hours of complete rest during the day if you bring it to work with you? I would advise health-care professionals to work with volunteer therapy dog handlers before taking any steps toward becoming handlers themselves. Many professionals can continue using volunteers indefinitely.

In this chapter you probably also expected to read which breeds are best suited as therapy dogs. Sorry! I could name breeds that are not usually suited, but that would be unfair to dogs of those breeds and their handlers who do qualify. Some people will respond only to therapy dogs that remind them of dogs they've known in the past. If we eliminate any dog without good reason, we eliminate help for those people. We may also eliminate a great volunteer in that dog's owner.

You might also assume that naturally friendly dogs are best suited, but that's only about half true. Friendliness and control are equally important, and both can be learned. The single most important factor is that the dog match the handler's ability.

Small dogs are easiest for beginners to handle, but they must be worked only with people who won't treat a dog roughly. That means there are some facilities in which you simply will not work with a small dog. In other facilities you may need to keep a small dog out of reach of some people, but it can be an excellent therapy dog.

With a large dog, control becomes an issue. Ideally, the dog should not be stronger than the handler. Using a dog you can physically restrain without violence will eliminate most of the need for neck jerks and other severe corrections that aren't acceptable in public. One measure of appropriate size is for the dog to weigh no more than one-third of what the handler weighs. By this standard, even a small woman can handle a dog big enough to work with most groups. If it takes a seventy-pound dog to work with a particular group, it will probably take an exceptional handler as well. With enough training though, a small person can handle a large dog—it's done all the time.

One disadvantage to using a dog you can't easily (and obviously) control is that people you visit might not have confidence that you can control the dog. You could find yourself constantly having to prove it. This defensive position is not conducive to good therapy dog work. The larger the dog, the more training both handler and dog need.

Some breeds or types of dog are better therapy candidates than others, but this is not an absolute rule. There are some general rules one should follow with the type of dog concerned. As an example, large strong dogs need firm control in therapy dog work. Training should be thorough and the dog dependable. Such dogs take training well and are generally better able to withstand physical stresses than smaller dogs.

The good work a therapy dog does is dramatic in a quiet way. As a result, sensational publicity tends to be out of place. When publicity can focus on a therapy dog's ability to communicate with learning impaired children, the elderly and the handicapped, it helps the whole image of this work and puts a bright, new glow on the world's oldest intraspecies compact. *Courtesy Dog Fancy Magazine*

Now we come to the question of male dogs versus female dogs. Obedience and aggressiveness vary from breed to breed and from dog to dog. Many male dogs make fine therapy dogs, especially if neutered around one year of age (as are male dogs that guide the blind). In general, however, female dogs are more obedient and less aggressive. Even docile male dogs can become targets for attack by other male dogs. In many cases, a female dog will represent the easier task for her therapy dog handler.

2.7. PUBLICITY

You've probably seen news articles and television stories about therapy dogs. Unfortunately, much of the media coverage doesn't represent the work very well. If you're serving faithfully as a therapy dog handler, you're working in quiet situations and are seldom in the limelight. When faced with the choice of doing a regularly scheduled visit with your dog or going for publicity, you'll choose faithfulness to those who love and need your dog. A therapy dog visit is not a show, although it may be entertaining; and though handlers certainly do educate, we do most of our work with people who can't take care of a dog themselves.

Therapy dog visits are often unexciting to watch. Some benefits to people are measured by the flicker of a hand, an eye or the corner of a mouth. It's a quiet, controlled activity that can quickly bore uninformed observers. Most of the miracles are simple, and even the exciting ones are often understood only by someone familiar with the person's medical history. Frequently the handler is never even told how the dog helped. Those who seek publicity for dog activities will find that entertainment and educational programs fit this criteria much better than therapy dog work does.

2.8. THE INDOOR DOG

The best place for a therapy dog to live is in the house. This requires commitment from the owner. A dog that lives in the house learns how to behave indoors with people, not to relieve itself indoors and how to tone down behavior inside. A house dog drools less. A dog's respiratory system actually changes after the dog spends as little as two weeks in a climate-controlled place. Drooling less is a big benefit for a therapy dog but a disadvantage for a dog that must work outdoors: it reduces the dog's ability to cool itself and can greatly reduce its stamina.

House dogs usually learn to walk on slick floors. If your house is completely carpeted or if your dog lives outdoors, be sure to find places for the dog to play on linoleum, ceramic tile and other slick surfaces regularly. You will encounter such floors in most facilities, and some dogs can't walk on them or fear them, due to lack of experience. Similarly, if your house has no stairs, find some for your dog to play on.

When my grandparents ran a household, most people lived in rural communities. Dogs that helped on the farm, like Mud, my grandmother's German shepherd dog, got dirty every day. People didn't have the products for parasite control that we have now. Farm families spent much of every day outdoors, so they were with their dogs. Mud slept outside my grandmother's bedroom window, which went all the way to the floor, so he could be near her at night.

Mud's heritage lives on in my dog Saint. But now I'm a city dweller, and Saint doesn't work cattle as Mud did. I pick up my yard every day, and Saint isn't dirty. I keep my yard and house free of fleas and ticks. There's no reason for Saint to have to watch over me through the bedroom window at night—his place is with me.

This depicts a typical change in generations. Our grandparents, who lived in a largely rural society, kept dogs outdoors for good reasons that don't apply to today's city dogs. They passed on to their children the knowledge that a dog is a trainable, working animal. Now, however, many dogs have to learn to live indoors in order to do their jobs, and to keep any dog-related complaints from neighbors to the barest minimum. Teaching your dog basic control (which I'll describe in a later chapter) and using the training every day will make it possible for you to live happily with your dog indoors. A therapy dog must be clean and well behaved enough for its owner's home before being taken into facilities where other people live and work.

2.9. PARASITE CONTROL

Therapy dogs must never carry fleas or ticks into a facility, and people could be harmed by pesticides on the dog when it comes to visit. The only practical solution is to consistently control fleas and

Because of the normal conditions at facilities therapy dogs visit, the indoor dog has the best chance of success as a trained therapy dog. Ingrained habits of cleanliness of the indoor dog and the ability to negotiate slippery surfaces are two of the many benefits.

ticks at home. Consult your veterinarian about pest control for your geographical area. Follow your veterinarian's directions exactly, since improper use of pesticides can kill your dog.

Wormers are just as dangerous as flea and tick products when used incorrectly. If your dog has worms, let your veterinarian prescribe the wormer and the dosage. It's not worth the risk of killing your dog to save a little money. You may also spend far more money and do far more work trying to get rid of parasites without proper information.

Proper care of your yard means picking up dog feces every day. Yes, every day! Pick up after the dog if it uses property outside your yard, too. This is the only way to avoid the risk of contaminating the soil. You might not know your dog has worms or a viral infection for quite some time; if you pick up every day, you greatly reduce the risk of transmitting problems to another dog—or reinfecting your own dog after treatment. The most convenient way to pick up is to put a plastic bag over your hand like a glove, pick up, invert the bag over the feces and discard. Since handlers also have to be prepared to pick up after their dogs on outings and at facilities, this is an essential skill to learn.

If you can't clean every day, do it without fail at least once a week. That, however, turns a simple job into a big one, and means a dirty yard between cleanings. The family gets less use of the yard, and the dog has less room to exercise and it will be hard for the dog to avoid the mess. Then you won't want the dog in the house.

2.10. THE VETERINARIAN

Visits to the veterinarian allow you to practice handling skills for when your dog is under stress and feeling mild pain. Working with the dog when discomfort is inevitable and a part of the dog's benefit is the only humane way for you to practice these skills. It's cruel to inflict pain on a dog for practice, and would damage your dog's confidence in you. Testing a dog by having others inflict pain on it could ruin the dog's trust in people. You could never fool the dog into thinking it was an accident. A dog *will* usually learn to realize that painful episodes on a therapy dog visit are purely accidental. Handling your dog during routine veterinary procedures is an opportunity you don't want to miss.

If you have a huge dog, you may not be able to hold it alone, and it may need to be attended to on the floor. For a smaller dog that gets care on the table, use both arms to hold the dog in a standing position. Wrap one arm around the dog's belly from underneath and the other around the dog's neck from underneath. Hold the dog against your body, and reach each hand as far around as you can, to keep the dog's head from turning back and to hold the dog steady. If necessary, encircle the dog's muzzle with your hand at the head. When possible, use that hand to scratch the dog behind its ears vigorously, which reduces sensations of pain elsewhere on the dog's body. Talk to the dog in a steady, pleasant voice on which the dog will learn to focus—this situation allows you to practice the skill of verbal encouragement.

Note how your dog reacts to pain and be honest about it. If your dog goes out of control when in pain, it shouldn't be a therapy dog.

Carry treats to the veterinarian's office, and encourage the doctor and assistants to use them. Let your dog get its treats from them, if possible. If your dog snaps at food, tell attendants in advance so they can offer the treats safely from the palms of their hands. It's messy but safe. A veterinarian's fingers are very important to him or her. You will likely find the veterinarian pleased to help with this, since it will make your dog easier for him or her to deal with not only during that office visit but in the future as well. The treats should be offered before anything uncomfortable is done as well as after. This orients the dog's attention to something pleasant. Use treats that won't make your dog sick, and small pieces so it can have several. If you forget, your veterinarian may have treats on hand.

If it's all right with your veterinarian, take the dog along on trips to the office when it won't be examined at all—to pay your bill, pick up supplies, etc. Don't expose the dog to sick dogs in the waiting room—go when the office is quiet. These trips help condition the dog not to fear the place.

You won't be an average dog owner. Your veterinarian will have to get to know you and how you manage your therapy dog. After you develop a good working relationship, you'll be able to do things at home for your therapy dog under the veterinarian's instructions that many dog owners can't do, which will save you money.

Your dog will have serious medical problems once in a while, and then a good veterinarian is your best ally. Some major medical problems can eliminate your dog from therapy dog work, while others won't. Get your veterinarian's help in deciding. Some illnesses require that your dog be isolated, or make the dog unusually pain-sensitive or irritable. In these cases a therapy dog must not work.

Your therapy dog, male or female, should ideally be neutered.

Bill Davis and Star demonstrate the restraint required during a veterinary examination: one arm under the belly, the other around the neck. The left hand scratches the dog's ear while the voice focuses her attention.

For the therapy dog, experiencing minor physical discomforts during the course of veterinary visits can often be good preparation for the well-intentioned, but not always harmless handling the dog would get from people it will encounter in some care facilities.

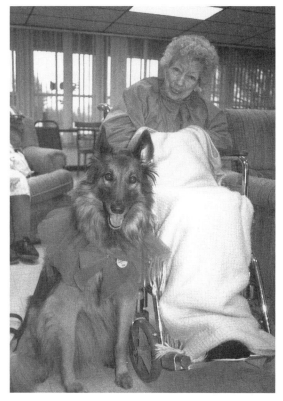

This isn't just something your dog has to go through to meet a requirement; neutering your dog will directly benefit it. Dogs are social animals and can have great closeness with one another without mating. Sexual relations don't mean the same things to dogs as to people. My three dogs are able to live happily together in a social unit because they are all neutered. Having a healthy social life with other dogs is good for a dog and good for its therapy dog work. Neutering allows your male or female dog to respond to you more consistently, especially in the presence of other dogs. It makes it safer for therapy dogs to have wide access to public places. It does not deprive your dog of its personality or its sexual identity, but does provide the dog with many health benefits. Don't hesitate to have your dog neutered—you're doing it a favor.

At some point an aging therapy dog may have to retire. Some dogs can do visits until the end of their lives—no one can predict. Watch the older dog for reduced tolerance of handling and for increased body sensitivity. When the dog no longer enjoys visits or begins to create health risks to people, the dog must stop.

You'll need to learn about care continually from your veterinarian, from other dog owners and from current dog magazines. It takes time to learn adequate care for your dog to be a therapy dog, and time to get a new dog's health and care routine stable, but excellent care is essential for a therapy dog.

2.11. IS THERAPY DOG WORK FOR YOU?

This is a good time to stop and think about what it means to be a therapy dog handler and whether it's what you want to do. Ask yourself some questions. Is this the way you want to live with your dog?

Dogs and people both become awkward with others if they stay alone too much—that's one of the reasons therapy dogs help people. This means that you can't just train the dog and have it permanently trained. You must practice throughout the dog's career to keep up both its skills and yours. It's a way of life.

Some people don't enjoy initiating social interaction with strangers. Your dog will be an enormous help in doing this, but you'll be the leader. If you don't like interacting with strangers, you might never enjoy being a therapy dog handler. Ask yourself whether this work fits your personality.

Handling a therapy dog does require a certain amount of talent and skill. Every therapy dog deserves the protection of a good handler. If you find that handling a therapy dog is not one of your talents, there are many other ways you can help therapy dog work. If you are a professional in a health-care facility, you can help to establish a program in the facility using volunteers and their dogs. If you own or manage a public place where health codes do not prohibit dogs, you can invite qualified therapy dog handlers to bring their dogs in regularly for social skills practice. If you produce stories for the news media, you can represent therapy dog work accurately. If you want to participate in therapy dog visits, you can go along to help stimulate people socially. If you are a veterinarian, you can give good advice to facilities and handlers, and arrange funding for any special tests facilities require on therapy dogs. If you teach obedience classes, you can spot, encourage and give special help to dog owners who want to learn therapy dog work. If you belong to a dog club, you can arrange classes and behavioral tests for therapy dogs and their handlers. If you live near a therapy dog handler, you can offer to help with training.

While handling a therapy dog is not for everyone, everyone has a role to play in providing therapy dog service to those who need it. Chances are you'll find your part a welcome addition to your life.

3

Visits as a Group

3.1. HELP HANDLERS GET STARTED

THE EASIEST WAY to start out as a therapy dog handler is usually to join a group. Joining a local group, a national group or a group of therapy dog handlers in a nearby community when your own community doesn't have one that's right for you can all be worthwhile options. The group will have standards to determine whether or not you and your dog qualify. Even if you aren't able to work directly with the group on visits, having them approve you provides a helpful credential.

Joining a group lets you find out if you enjoy this work and if you and your dog are suited for it. It can give you a chance to try therapy dog work without getting people in a facility attached to your dog before you're sure you want to make a commitment.

If after talking to a group's leader you feel you might be interested in joining, the first step is to attend a practice session. Don't bring your dog the first time, simply come to observe. Do you feel comfortable with the way they treat dogs? Do you feel that you and your dog would be safe around these dogs? If so, talk to the leader about bringing your dog to a future session. The group leader will want to observe your dog in practice before letting you bring it on a therapy dog visit.

Many groups don't have practice sessions, but members may attend competition obedience training classes together. There would probably be a few therapy dog handlers there, along with many dog trainers not involved in therapy dog work. In such a situation it may be hard to judge how the group works on actual therapy dog visits. Obedience classes stress precision, which is different from the controlled sociability of therapy dog visits.

The next step is to attend a therapy dog visit with the group, without bringing your dog. This will give you a chance to observe the group in a facility. If you're unsure after this first visit, don't bring your dog as the next step. Instead, attend more visits as an observer, in different types of facilities.

If you feel uncomfortable around people with disabilities or in nursing homes or other facilities, this doesn't necessarily mean you wouldn't enjoy working there with a therapy dog. Many volunteers do a few visits and quit. Sometimes that's a mistake. Most of us with empathy for other people feel uncomfortable in a situation where people seem to be suffering. Three things may help you overcome this:

1. Give yourself three, four or more visits before making a decision. Like our dogs, we often get used to a situation with experience. Don't give up too soon.

2. Investigate possibilities for an orientation through a local nursing home or other facility similar to the one in which you want to work. Since these feelings are so common, some facilities have people who can help volunteers cope with them.

3. Learn your job as a therapy dog handler. When you develop the needed skills and can turn your attention to working your dog with people in the facility, you'll find your body and mind redirected from the things that used to bother you. You'll also find yourself surrounded by the good you and your dog do. The atmosphere around you will become positive and happy. As you adjust to the situation, you'll often realize that the people aren't suffering as much as you thought they were. In nursing homes, for example, people may be distressed for the first two weeks, then adjust to their new lifestyles. Any therapist will tell you that oversympathizing with people interferes with your ability to help them.

Besides giving yourself the opportunity to try the work, starting out with a group often means working under someone capable of

For the person considering volunteering for therapy dog work, it is important to talk to experienced volunteers, attend practice sessions and observe the real interaction of dogs and people in facilities before making a firm committment. *Courtesy Dog Fancy Magazine*

It is normal for some people to feel uncomfortable around people with impairments. While there is no need to feel ashamed of this, it is possible to overcome such a response if therapy dog work is what you want to do. Often, getting immersed in the work gives the handler a new, positive perspective.

controlling a dog obedience class. On the first few visits, this person can be a great help. He or she can objectively evaluate you and your dog, give an opinion as to whether you're ready to do visits (before you go on the first one) and then observe your work on visits and let you know how you're doing. He or she can usually prevent problems that might arise from bringing a group of dogs together, mostly by well-timed reminders to handlers to watch their dogs.

If you have doubts about your dog's behavior, don't start therapy dog visits. But even if you think you and your dog are ready, it's wise to start with a skilled instructor present.

3.2. AGGRESSIVE DOGS

Working with a group of dogs calls attention to the point of a therapy dog's ability to get along with other dogs. Dogs that fight with other dogs can be a danger to people as well as to their own kind. Experts familiar with such dogs should probably be consulted to determine when a dog with this propensity is adequately trained to function as a therapy dog. Don't assume that if your untrained dog likes to fight with other dogs you can still do therapy dog work with that dog by doing visits on your own instead of with a group. You'll eventually encounter other dogs. When a facility allows one therapy dog, it's likely to allow others, including such untrained dogs as the pets of family members visiting people who live in the facility. The fact that the other dog may have started it won't matter a bit if you can't control your dog in the situation.

A dog fight presents one of the greatest risks of injury to people posed by the presence of dogs. The dogs seldom intend to bite people—which is why some people don't consider dogs that fight with other dogs dangerous—but people get between the fighting dogs and are bitten. This has gotten many owners bitten by their own dogs. When Star was being attacked, I knew the sensible action would have been to leave her to her fate, but she was screaming in fear and I could not. So I held her in the air and screamed ''Help!'' until the other dog's owners heard and called their dog. I was bruised, bitten and traumatized. It gave me even more respect than before for the feelings of those who fear dogs—that fear is not without reason.

Most therapy dogs are treasured. Not only do the owners love their dogs, people in facilities become attached to therapy dogs as well. Injury to a therapy dog would hurt these people, and it would

The therapy dog must be trustworthy around other dogs as well as around people. That is why part of therapy dog training includes meeting and interacting with other dogs in a purely non-aggressive context.

take a long time to train a new dog to replace the working ability of this therapy dog. A traumatic attack from an aggressive dog could ruin a fine dog's attitude and behavior toward other dogs. I was blessed that Star, who has a very soft and submissive temperament, came out of the experience believing that I had rescued her. She has always been submissive toward other dogs and still is, with no inclination to fight with them out of fear. She shows much more faith than I sometimes feel.

A therapy dog visit has a different atmosphere from a dog training class or show event. Some aggressive dogs that can function well in a class or a competitive setting can't function safely in a therapy setting. While no therapy dog should be wandering around the room without handler supervision, different dogs may touch each other at times during visits.

For this reason I like to introduce my dog to any new dog while the handler's attention is on the dog, and before we start visiting with people. This gives the dogs a good look at each other, and lets both handlers remind the dogs that growling or other signs of aggression won't be tolerated. Do this only with full cooperation from other handlers. They know their dogs and their own handling capabilities.

This is a good time to point out the importance of an attentive handler. An inattentive handler doesn't even know which dog is growling. I remember a small male poodle in obedience class that took every opportunity to growl at Saint, at which point the handler would glare at me. Saint was interested in sniffing the poodle, which I didn't let him do, but he never growled at it or wished it any harm. The other dog owner never seemed to realize her dog was the one growling. How easy it would have been for her to let the dog know she would not tolerate it. All it takes is correcting the dog the instant it growls, and then praising the dog the next time it's around the other dog and does not growl. With firmness from her, and the safety net of Saint's good nature, that trainer could have taught her dog a valuable lesson.

When your dog gets used to your consistent attention, it will also more readily leave it to you to deal with other dogs. If you neglect to watch and properly direct your dog, the dog may decide it must take over the job of "protecting" you from other dogs. In reality, a dog that fights with other dogs puts its owner in danger.

If your dog shows any aggression toward other dogs, you must solve the problem before attempting therapy dog work. You must also be very sure you are skilled enough and strong enough to control the dog.

3.3. STANDARDS, UNINTERRUPTED SERVICE TO FACILITIES

A major service that a therapy dog group can perform is to establish standards for therapy dog work in a community. If facilities learn that when they call this group, dogs and handlers will do consistent, problem-free visits, the group will develop a good reputation.

Therapy dog groups are often affiliated with either obedience training organizations or animal welfare organizations. Some animal welfare organizations use trained dogs for visits, while others don't. You may not want to take your dog on visits with other dogs that are untrained or have come straight from an animal shelter without a quarantine period. Animal welfare organizations are increasingly convinced of the value of training to solve dog problems and to make dogs more secure in their homes. However, they're often offended by harsh dog training. Since therapy dog training shouldn't be harsh and is exactly right for many animal shelter dogs, I hope that animal welfare organizations will increasingly sponsor training to help the dogs they place and to produce more therapy dogs. Both goals can be achieved through one curriculum.

Another important service that a therapy dog group can provide is to make sure a facility has continuous therapy dog visits. If one handler quits, the group can send out another. Similarly, if there's a problem with the handler, the facility can contact the group leader and let the group deal with the problem. This puts experienced trainers and handlers on the job, instead of leaving a facility staff member to criticize a volunteer without, perhaps, any real solution to offer. Training and working dogs is a technical skill that most people don't have.

Training groups tend to use well-behaved dogs. If your dog has problems, a training group may help you—trainers view most problems as having solutions.

3.4. INSURANCE

All therapy dog groups should consider getting insurance. This is especially true of groups that accept fees from handlers or facilities. Volunteers are less likely to be sued. For the volunteer therapy dog handler who does not accept money for doing visits, personal liability insurance may suffice. Your homeowner's or renter's policy may provide this. It does not cover professional dog work.

A group accepting money has additional liability that may require insurance. If a group sends a dog out on a visit and someone claims that harm was done, the group might be sued for not adequately screening the dog and handler. The handler's insurance and the facility's insurance protect their respective liabilities but not the group's.

The risks in this activity are extremely low when common sense and handler attention are applied. The rate of negative incidents is especially low with trained dogs working with qualified volunteer owners. The highest rate of accidents occur with dogs living in facilities and working without handlers.

Local groups may want to handle insurance liability by registering all dogs with one of the national therapy dog registeries that provide insurance. This will also cover personal liability for handlers who do not have adequate insurance. Another alternative would be for groups not to certify dogs, but rather to serve as associations of handlers who assume responsibility for their own dogs.

Belonging to a group gives some handlers a false sense of security. Please realize that you're no less responsible for your dog's behavior when with a group than when working alone. Your liability is the same as in any situation with your dog—the law holds the owner responsible for the dog's behavior.

3.5. WORKING WITH FACILITY STAFF

Facility staff members can have quite a problem locating volunteers to do therapy dog visits. A therapy dog group probably won't have an office, although some who are affiliated with animal welfare or other organizations may. When there's no office, one person will need to take calls from facilities and do the scheduling. It doesn't work well to change this job around among group members, because facilities won't be able to keep up with the changing phone numbers.

Local groups function in various ways. Some send out individual dogs and handlers, so that even though you belong to a group, you do one-dog visits. Others always send multiple dogs and handlers. Because there are so many ways of doing therapy dog visits, try to consider more than one group and join the one that fits you best. In a group, the leader usually works with the facility to set up visits. If the leader isn't present at every visit, a member who is there will need to understand the group's way of working and be able to communicate with the staff.

Sometimes the staff will forget the dogs are coming. If you're doing a one-dog visit, this may not be a big problem, except for depriving the people of the benefit of something to look forward to. It's more of a problem when a group of handlers and dogs visits. Since it's possible that your visit has been forgotten, the first qualified person to reach the facility should go in and let someone know the dogs are arriving. This person needs to be capable of explaining to the staff how to set up for the visit, in case the contact person in the facility is unexpectedly absent. In all dealings with the facility staff, handlers need to be businesslike, use courtesy, and keep a positive attitude. Staff people are used to dealing with volunteers, but they have to trust therapy dog handlers in a special way. If you seem to have a personality problem, they may be reluctant to let you bring a dog into the facility.

If you have trouble with a staff person, don't indulge your feelings—others are probably having trouble with that person, too. The problem will usually get solved without your help, or the staff person will find another job. Avoid going to someone's superior if you can, because that often greatly increases problems. When his or her superior says you complained, the staff member may become much more negative toward you than before. However, you may have to take this risk if the problem is serious.

You may encounter a staff person who's hostile to dogs. If the whole facility doesn't want you, don't push. Wait to be invited. If they're hostile, they won't support your work. It's better to go to one of the many facilities who are already sold on the concept of therapy dogs and are seeking volunteers.

But once the facility does invite you, don't try to make a case for therapy dogs with a negative staff person by arguing, just do your job with your dog. You'll see an amazing thing happen—the dog's nonverbal abilities and your good handling will work on them. Over time you'll see them respond to your therapy dog, nonverbally at first. Eventually their words will change, too. Sometimes the formerly hostile people become the most enthusiastic about your work!

Therapy dog work isn't done with words. Let the work "speak" for itself. It's far more powerful than any words you could use. It also takes time. Flawless behavior in the facility with your dog will buy you that time. Never force the dog on anyone. Don't try to argue people out of their fears. The antidote to fear is to replace it with love. Your therapy dog has what it takes to do that.

3.6. INDOOR OR OUTDOOR VISITS?

One important question about therapy dog visits is whether to work indoors or outdoors at the facility. I do all visits indoors, except special events when everyone is outside. The weather in my area wouldn't allow for consistent outdoor visits. Wind, rain and temperatures are unpredictable and extreme. Outdoor visits will often eliminate some of the people in the facility from participation. They can also expose the dogs to dangerous heat, internal parasites, fleas, ticks and stray dogs, depending on the location.

In some areas the conditions do allow for outdoor therapy dog visits. Group leaders and individual handlers need to decide whether to work outdoors or not. If the facility wants you outdoors because they don't trust the dogs, you'll have to decide whether to win their trust with good work outdoors, or suggest that they call back later if they can arrange indoor therapy dog visits. If you have a trained therapy dog, the ideal place for visits is indoors. When the situation is looser, with dogs not groomed for the indoors or with puppies, that session—not one that could accurately be called a therapy dog visit—may belong outdoors.

3.7. EDUCATION, ENTERTAINMENT OR THERAPY?

Each group should set goals for visits. This allows group members to function in harmony and lets them clearly explain to facilities what they have to offer.

Training clubs and other dog organizations may want to concentrate on entertainment combined with petting at nursing homes and education combined with petting for schools and civic groups.

Therapy dog work isn't done with words... It's far more powerful than any words you can use.

The program for visits will depend on whether or not the group can practice together, on the training of the dogs, and on the priorities of the group. When visits are done regularly to each facility served, performance becomes unnecessary. Regular visits let people get to know and love the dogs as individuals, which is more therapeutic than doing a show.

When a group is unable to offer regular service to any one facility, but instead spreads visits among many facilities, or is able to do only a few visits a year, a brief presentation of obedience work and tricks will provide a stimulating social experience for people, reassure everyone that the dogs are safe to have there and encourage petting. People will feel more at ease petting the dogs after seeing them perform. This may be the most practical approach for obedience clubs that also conduct training classes and sponsor competitive events. Such a club may not be the ideal therapy dog group, however, since it can't offer consistent service or facilities. Show seasons interrupt service, and volunteers may be able to participate only when visits don't interfere with show work. On the other hand, this is ideal as a means of introducing trained dogs to the community and giving new handlers an introduction to therapy dog work. Such groups should be encouraged as a much-needed link between obedience training clubs and therapy dog work.

3.8. COOPERATION AMONG GROUPS

Since many different kinds of groups do therapy dog visits, friction can arise between groups. There's actually no need for competition. On the contrary, there are several reasons for groups to cooperate. There is certainly enough work for everyone.

Facilities learn about the benefits of therapy dog visits through their professional organizations. They meet with each other locally and at national conferences, and they receive professional publications that feature animal-assisted therapy. Universities and other organizations are studying animal-assisted therapy. This is creating a growing demand for therapy dogs.

Many facilities have tried unsuccessfully to have resident dogs. They've tried having puppies brought in. They've tried dogs that have been through a screening process but are either untrained or handled by children. These programs sometimes work, but may cause safety concerns and staff complaints. A trained therapy dog brought to visit by a qualified volunteer handler meets the needs of almost all facilities. When they learn that is what you have to offer, your services will be much in demand. This may take time—two or three years isn't unusual. But once it happens, you'll probably have more requests for visits than you can fill. At that point, you'll need to refer callers to other therapy dog handlers.

Another reason to refer a facility is when they're too far away. Many handlers and dogs travel long distances to do visits, and while this may be necessary in communities where everything is spread out, in general the shorter the trip to and from the facility, the more energy handler and dog will have for the visit. Transportation costs are reduced, visits can be done more consistently in marginal weather and handlers feel stronger commitments to facilities in their own neighborhoods.

Cultivating good relations with other groups in your area can allow you to exchange volunteers. Sometimes a volunteer lives nearer another group or has preferences that better suit a different group's goals. If you have good communication and cooperation, you can refer these people to the best groups for them and conserve volunteers who would otherwise be lost.

Some groups may be able to offer training programs, but many won't. Therapy dog groups in an area could work together to help volunteers find training. Seminars to inform area dog-training instructors about therapy dog work would be an inexpensive way for groups to improve area therapy dog training.

Cooperation among groups is important if the public is to trust the concept of trained therapy dogs. This is important nationally, as well, because negative perceptions about therapy dogs could make insurance a problem. This will not happen if people stick to the facts: insurance companies have nothing to fear from the work of trained therapy dogs working with handlers. Injuries rarely occur.

3.9. DOES THIS GROUP MAKE YOU PROUD?

The last consideration for a handler in deciding whether or not to join a particular group is whether this group makes you proud to be a part of it. That's a decision each handler has to make, and many things go into it. You need to share the group's goals and you need to feel satisfied with the competence of the other handlers. Your safety and your dog's, as well as your reputation and even your dog's life, may depend on their behavior.

No one handler can do everything. The more you learn about the dizzying variety of dog activities available, the more you'll realize that you have to make choices. My choice has been to get to know and stay in touch with as many handlers as possible but—after originally starting with a local group—to do therapy dog visits on my own now, with one dog at a time. Whatever choice you make, you will benefit from group ties.

4

Visits with One Dog

4.1. GREATER RESPONSIBILITY

Doing THERAPY DOG VISITS as an individual handler with one dog is a greater responsibility than working with a group. If you quit after having visited enough times for people to bond with the dog, you may harm someone. Your abandonment of a facility where people have become attached to your dog would probably not cause as much grief as a pet owner losing a pet, but it would still have negative effects on vulnerable people.

It also takes time for the staff to get used to you. Bringing a therapy dog program into a facility can be a complicated process. Someone may have worked hard to get the administration's permission. If you quit, the facility faces starting over with a new volunteer. They may give up the idea.

This would be a loss to other therapy dog volunteers, too, because generally handlers can't call facilities and be quickly accepted as volunteers. It's like applying for a job, since the facility will be at least partly responsible for your actions while you volunteer there. By causing a facility to become discouraged about working with therapy dog handlers, you may close the door to other volunteers looking for places to serve. When a handler who does visits alone needs to stop, that person should try hard to find a reliable volunteer and dog to take over the job.

If you commence therapy dog visits as an individual at a facility, be prepared to continue those visits. Discontinuing your therapy work could easily undo all the benefits you have brought to a facility.

With the added responsibility of working as an individual handler, however, also comes great freedom. When working a dog on my own in a facility, I can do things I can't do when working with the group. My dogs and I don't have the constant pressure of other dogs, and I have more flexibility to work with people. My dogs work in familiar settings, going back regularly to the same facilities, and even though my sessions are longer now, they show less fatigue than when I did visits to lots of different facilities with lots of other handlers and dogs.

Visits with one dog differ profoundly from therapy dog visits with a group of dogs, yet both kinds of visits have advantages. Working with therapy dogs offers a rich variety of experiences for any handler, with lots of choices to find the work you'll most enjoy.

4.2. WIN APPROVAL OF A GROUP

Because it's such a big responsibility to serve a facility on your own, it's usually best to stay in a group until you're sure you want to make a serious commitment to therapy dog work. When a handler decides to start doing visits alone, these group ties will help. Many groups receive requests from facilities for visits they can't fit into their schedules. Once the leader feels you're qualified, you can probably be given some of these referrals. Don't expect this to happen quickly. Reputation is important in therapy dog work.

Starting with a group will also screen your dog for working around other dogs. Even on one-dog visits, you will eventually encounter other dogs in facilities. However, unlike group visits with other skilled dog trainers present, you may be the only one there who knows what can happen when two dogs meet and what to do to prevent problems. The other dog could be a resident pet, a family pet brought to visit, or a stray in the parking lot. Even if the dog has a handler, the handler may not be able to control the dog. The two dogs might get along, but even normal canine responses could cause them to bump into people and caused someone to fall.

You and your dog must be at least as good with other dogs to do one-dog visits as to do visits with a group of other handlers and dogs. Gaining this skill is one of many things starting out your therapy dog visits with a group can do for you.

4.3. WORKING WITH THE STAFF

One aspect of working on my own that I particularly enjoy is working with the staff. As a member of a group, you might not schedule visits and work closely with the staff. When you work on your own, you take over these duties. In the process, you learn more about how the facility benefits from your visits than when you have a group leader. I like this communication with the staff and use it on every visit. While I try to be considerate of their time, I value these opportunities to get more feedback from them. When you visit each facility at least once a month and deal directly with the staff on each visit, you can learn more about how to improve your work for that facility's needs.

You also hear the negative things! Because volunteers are so important to facilities, staff will word any complaints tactfully. But complaints will come to you directly instead of going through the group leader (unless your one-dog visits are under the organization of a group). I like this chance to work problems out directly.

When a group of dogs visits a facility, the staff may not be able to provide a staff person to work with each handler and dog. But when you come on a visit with one dog, some facilities will have a staff person work with the people as you handle the dog. This is my favorite way to work. Not only do people derive maximum benefits from visits with strong staff support, but I get more feedback and learn more—which makes me a better handler. I want to grow in this work. I never expect to know it all.

Many staff members don't understand therapy dog work. You may need to encourage them to participate in your visits. So many entertainment programs have been done with dogs that the staff may assume you do that type of program, too. If you want to work differently, tell them. The staff can't give your visits the proper support unless you communicate with them.

All of this means you must be good at dealing with the staff in order for visits on your own to work well. If you need help with this aspect of therapy dog visits, working with a group will provide that for you.

Working as an individual handler with one dog offers a level of freedom not generally possible with a group. There are different advantages and drawbacks to working alone or with others. The beginning handlers should probably work with a group. When he and his dog acquire the polish that comes with experience, single visits can be more successful.

A therapy dog visit by a skilled handler with one dog has all the benefits associated with the work, but does not disrupt or conflict with the day's routine.

4.4. QUIETER, LESS DISRUPTION TO FACILITY ROUTINE

One thing staff members like about one-dog visits is that, if the handler is skilled, such visits cause little disruption to the facility's routine. Some people in facilities may insist on postponing care to spend time with the dog, but that's balanced by those who cooperate better with staff for the rest of the day after the dog's visit. If you don't do a show, the visit is even quieter. A show gives staff a "hook" to get people out of their rooms, but it also requires time to bring everyone out at once and to take them back. If you visit quietly in one or more central areas of the facility for an hour or so, staff can bring people out a few at a time, sometimes on the way to or from care. If you go to rooms, one dog causes less interference with facility routine than having several dogs and handlers visiting rooms in the facility at once.

Whether you do one-dog visits or group visits is for the handler and the facility to decide. The excitement of visits when a group of dogs is in the facility also creates benefits for people. Each type of program has advantages.

4.5. STRONGER FOCUS

Giving a focal point to people such as those with Alzheimer's disease and children with learning disabilities works best when only one dog is in the room. When more than one dog is present, people's attention can flit from one dog to another, and it can take longer to deal both with people's fear of dogs and to get on to therapy.

4.6. LIMITS

A major difference between group and individual visits is the number of people you can serve. You can do a performance in front of a large group with only one dog. However, if you want to let the people pet and interact with the dog, too large a group of people leaves many with nothing to do while you work the dog with a few at a time.

It's best for a person to have at least fifteen minutes with the dog if he or she shows strong interest. Just running quickly around

A stronger focus can be achieved when only one therapy dog visits at a time. This is especially beneficial for those with Alzheimer's disease or with learning impaired children.

the room for petting gives little opportunity for true therapy. Three or four people can sometimes share that fifteen-minute session, but some people will need the dog all to themselves.

A good guideline when starting out is to limit visits to about an hour and the number of people the dog works with to about a dozen. You may need to limit a small dog to fewer people, and a large dog may comfortably work with more people. Experience will teach you how to set limits.

You must consider setting limits for performances as well. On a group visit with other dogs and handlers, your dog might do some of the performances and rest during much of it. On a one-dog visit, your dog has to do the whole show. This cuts into its stamina for interaction with people.

Going from room to room is tiring for the dog, too. One therapy dog group has suggested that the dog work in no more than four rooms on a visit. This is realistic.

4.7. ROOMS VERSUS MEETING AREAS

When working on your own, it's up to you to decide with the staff where in the facility you and the dog will work. It will help you to know some of the pluses and minuses about different ways of setting up the visit.

I want a staff person to be available at all times on my therapy dog visits. This is easiest for nursing homes to provide if you work in a central area or next to a nursing station. If they can't provide a staff member to work directly with you, at least in these locations you can hail one.

Why this criteria? One experience crystallized it for me. I was in a room with my small spitz, Angel, when a disoriented woman clutched the little dog and began to squeeze, hard. The lady clearly wasn't going to let go and was hurting Angel. The facility's social services director was working with me. While I worked Angel as if she were having a veterinary procedure done—keeping her attention focused on my voice, and scratching behind her ears—the staff member gently pried the woman's hands loose. Angel wasn't injured or upset. She didn't bite the woman, or even offer to. No harm done. Would it have turned out that way if I'd been in the room without help? I don't want to find out.

The handler must be able to control the dog, but the staff has

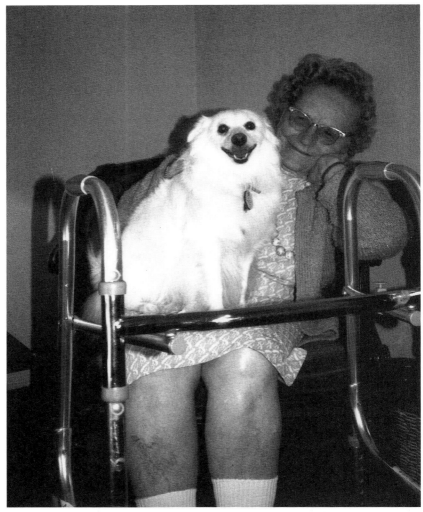

When you are familiar with the facilities you visit and with the reactions of your fully trained dog, you can determine the best format for your visits. The results you aim for are well-illustrated by the two faces here.

to control the people. Staff should tell the handler if a particular person might abuse the dog, and should remain available to step in and control people who might get rough. The therapy dog handler is usually not a therapist, and the handler's attention must be focused on the dog. I'm not saying you would be wrong to visit rooms without a staff person. It's something you need to decide. I make exceptions for people I know.

Because I do want a staff person present, I often find that if a nursing home doesn't have anyone available, I'm more comfortable in central areas with people who come out of their rooms. This also allows staff members to bring people to see the dog, since they know where the dog will be.

In nursing homes, therapy dog handlers are often routed through the Social Services or Activities departments. The more consistent you are about your visits, the more the nursing staff will get involved. This means more benefits to people, because nurses and other caretakers work more closely with people and know their specific therapeutic needs better than the social staff does. To get strong staff support for your visits, be consistent and keep communication open.

You can combine working in rooms with working in central areas, and many handlers do. I usually work in common areas unless I have requests to go to particular rooms, or a staff member visits rooms with me. Another option is to go to rooms before or after working your dog in a central area. Groups often do this.

You can stick to room visits and not work in common areas at all—though you will probably find yourself stopping in halls and common areas on the way to and from the rooms you visit, to work with others who want to see the dog. You may develop relationships with certain people and go straight to their rooms. After you know them, having a staff person there may become unimportant.

4.8. MAKING CHANGES

Your wishes about how you want to work will change as you learn and as you work with different dogs. Staff members change what they want from you, too, and staff people leave their jobs and are replaced. There are many opportunities to change your routine.

One of the hardest changes for me has been to move from doing shows to having interactions with people without a performance. My dogs are good performers, and people enjoy that. The staff got into the habit of bringing everyone out for a show and coming back to get them when the show was over. If you start your work in a facility by doing shows, it can be difficult to change the routine. The staff may not realize that interaction with the dog is more therapeutic for people, especially if staff members stay busy doing other things when you're there and don't get involved in therapy dog visits.

Another problem comes when, in order to get people out of their rooms, the staff has told them the dog is going to do tricks. If you have one dog and the staff has assembled thirty people, how can you include them all except by doing a performance? You can get stuck in this situation. If you prefer to have more interaction with people and want to eliminate performance work once you've started it, you'll need the staff's help. They'll need to stop bringing a large group out at once, and start telling people that you and your dog are coming to visit, not to do tricks. At one facility I visit, it had been the custom for the desk person, seeing a dog arrive, to announce over the public address system that there would be a dog show and for everyone to come out. We had to get him to stop doing this when he saw Angel.

At an adult day-care facility I visit, the day is filled with activities to stimulate people, a primary function of the program. When I did therapy dog visits at 10:30 A.M., they needed short, snappy presentations for the whole group at once. That didn't allow much interaction between participants and the dog. I inquired about changing our time to early morning, when the facility opens. Now I get there with the dog at 7:30 A.M., and visit quietly with people as they arrive. When they start the first program in midmorning, the dog and I leave. Everyone seems happy with the change.

4.9. THE APPROACH

Particularly in nursing homes, handlers encounter people who, when asked if they would like to pet the dog, immediately say no. Sometimes it's the first choice people have had all day, and they reject the dog just to feel some control over their lives. Unfortunately, this not only makes the handler feel rejected, but also deprives the person being visited from enjoying and benefiting from the dog.

People will also say no because they misunderstand the question, because they don't want to monopolize the dog or because they

People in a care facility who would be receptive to a visit from your therapy dog don't have to say so. Often their body language will signal their attraction and your dog will surely be able to pick up on these cues.

feel self-conscious with the group's attention on them. As a handler you can often turn these "no" answers into "yes" answers, but you must respect people's wishes, and your time is limited. You might want to try my tactic. I don't ask "Would you like to pet the dog," instead, I read people's body language and occasionally ask "Do you like dogs?" I bring the dog near those people who seem attracted to it. I also take cues from the staff—they often know which people do or do not want the dog near.

To encourage petting, I pet the dog myself and say, "He (or she) likes to be petted." If two or three people are with the dog, I let them know that the dog enjoys being petted by more than one person at once. My dogs will often turn their backs for petting. I need to tell people what the dog is doing, or some think the dog doesn't like them! The back or the back of the head can be exactly the right part of the dog to offer to some people for petting, especially nervous young children.

Your personality will determine your approach to people. I prefer to approach quietly and avoid triggering rejection. Other handlers may enjoy a more overt and exciting approach. This approach can be stimulating to people, and for some it works best. When you work with staff people, they may make the approach instead of you, which gives you opportunities to experience different styles. As long as you are courteous and respect everyone's feelings, the best approach to use is the one that makes you most comfortable. With experience, you will probably build a repertoire of ways to approach different types of people. This comes with time. Meanwhile, no one should push a new handler. Let each handler's individual style develop naturally, at a pace that leaves the handler confident of control over the dog.

4.10. WORKING WITH CHILDREN

One facility I serve is a school for children with disabilities, where performance plays a different role. Preschool-age children are striving to develop mental and social skills, and having the dog perform helps them progress. We'll probably always include some demonstration work and tricks for that reason, and to help them form an understanding of working dogs. These demonstrations for the children are brief, but when I see four or five groups in a morning, that's a lot of demonstrating! However, I've found ways to relieve

If your therapy dog is to work with children, be especially careful about the extremely fearful or severely allergic child. Make certain also that the dog is not placed under undue stress in working with children.

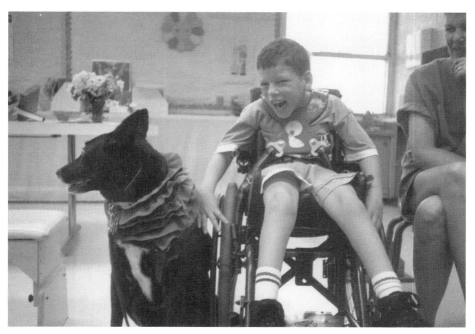

Therapy dogs have achieved amazing breakthroughs in reaching those once thought completely unreachable.

stress on the dog. One way to help the dog is to have it stationed in one room and the children brought to that room. Working in "its own" room, the dog settles in and is spared the stress of adjusting to a new environment for each group.

If the dog is hot or thirsty, I stop at any time during a visit or presentation to offer water (people love to see the dog receive this care), but the break between groups is another chance for the dog to drink. If the dog has been pushed a bit too hard by a group, the break lets me give it some tennis balls to chase, or some other diversion to forget the negative experience.

Keeping the dog out of classrooms benefits the children and the school. If a child is severely afraid of dogs or allergic to them, it's best not to put that child into a room with the dog. If the dog were to visit the classroom, the allergic child would be exposed not only during the visit, but also after the dog left, since allergens from the dog would linger.

If the school unknowingly brings an allergic child to the dog in a room that isn't his or her regular classroom, the exposure is limited to the time of the visit. The child goes back to the classroom in a few minutes, and any allergic reaction is sure to be lessened. Preferably, allergic children stay in the classroom with a teacher while others come to see the dog. Childhood allergies can be life threatening, so please do not overlook this risk.

Children who are too difficult to handle can also remain in the classroom. The teachers know which children might get out of control. Having the visit outside the classroom gives teachers this important option.

Fearful children should not be pressured at all. If they don't come into the session with the dog, they'll still hear about it from classmates. Over a period of time, they'll develop a desire to come see the dog. If they still don't like the dog near them, keep a distance. Let them watch for as many visits as they wish. What they'll see is a dog always under a handler's control, interacting with their happy classmates. It is almost certain that over time they will overcome their fear and will want to pet the dog. This is how it should happen—not by pushing them to accept the dog in one session.

Also, be aware that some children go through a developmental fear period about dogs. With good dog experiences and no bad ones, they often outgrow this. This fear may or may not involve a previous bad experience with a dog.

4.11. FIRST VISITS AWKWARD

Expect your first three or four visits to any facility to be awkward. The staff doesn't know how to work with you yet, the people may be uncertain about the dog, bonds take time to form and you may not know at first exactly how you want to work in that facility. Things get a lot smoother after the first few visits, and they continue to get better and better. Once they realize you're going to keep coming, staff members will work with you more and people will respond to you and the dog more. This takes time, because many volunteers don't last, and you have to show them that you will. There's no better way to show your commitment than by putting in the time.

Most studies of therapy dog work have been based on short-term study projects, not consistent long-range programs. I think there will be even more evidence of benefits to people when long-term visits by the same dog and handler are followed by researchers. I see improvements at one year, at two years, and the improvements continue after that. Not only does it get better the longer you do it, you enjoy it more, too.

4.12. THE LEASH

You may find that you'll work your dog off leash more on one-dog visits than on group visits, but this must be a moment-by-moment decision. A handler has to constantly assess risks. The leash should be on unless there is a good reason to have it off. The dog should never be off leash unless that dog is just as reliable off leash as on leash. Most dogs and handlers will never have that much control.

A handler doing a one-dog visit might feel a false sense of security with no other dogs there. But what if another dog unexpectedly arrives? I've had that experience more than once. Even if no other dog comes, do you have enough off-leash control over your dog to keep it from bumping or tripping a fragile person, or a staff member rushing to an emergency? Are you familiar enough with the facility routine and traffic patterns to see someone coming and move your loose dog in time?

Whenever a therapy dog on a visit with its handler isn't wearing a physical leash, there must be a flawless ''mental leash'' between dog and handler. If you're not absolutely sure you have that, keep the leash on. Also always keep it on when the rules require it, or when you're asked to do so.

5

Conditioning the Dog to Handling

A THERAPY DOG MUST HAVE plenty of hands-on touching, in training and thoughout its working life. We need every possible tool for working with the dog. Lots of time spent conditioning the dog to touch and other handling becomes a tremendous asset when teaching the dog anything, including commands.

5.1. THE MOTIVATORS: FOOD, PRAISE, PETTING AND PLAY

You have four main tools to motivate your dog to do as you ask. The first is *food*. Food is popular among professional trainers as well as pet owners. Food also has an important place in therapy dog work. It's helpful in teaching young puppies and it's a good attention-getter, to direct the dog's attention without using force. It can help you get a dog to try something new that it is reluctant to do and food can help you relate to a dog that doesn't know you well.

While food can relax a dog and help direct its attention, it is not a strong motivator unless the dog is quite hungry. A dog that must be fasted and worked on food is not ready to be a therapy dog.

The therapy dog must be in a sound and composed physical, mental and emotional state when it goes on a visit.

The second motivator is *praise*. Praise can't be overdone, except perhaps by praising a dog for such dangerous instincts as aggression toward people or animals. Even then, it's letting the dog carry out such instincts that does most of the harm. Expressing an instinct frequently makes it stronger, which is a problem for dogs with instincts that would be best kept dormant.

The pure form of praise uses voice and body language, without touch. The more you talk to your dog and note its reactions, the more you'll learn how to talk to that dog in a manner it enjoys. You'll also learn how to use your voice to tell the dog you're displeased, to give a verbal command or to encourage the dog to keep working. When necessary, you'll know how to make a lifeline of your voice to hold your dog steady under stress.

Dogs learn body language more easily than they learn words, and a good handler learns to notice and control his or her movements. Since your dog will be aware of every detail, you can use your body language with verbal language or in situations where your dog can't hear you to convey messages.

Sensitivity to the uses of both verbal and body language should therefore be cultivated to the highest degree in a therapy dog. This takes time and requires spending as much of it as possible with your dog. In this way, keeping the dog in the house with you is a great help.

The more effort you make to respond to a dog's communication, the more the dog will work to do the same for you. Many owners who think their dogs are stupid have probably not given them enough attention or encouragement to teach them to communicate. If a child were as understimulated as many dogs are, the child would show the same mental dullness. Bright, responsive dogs are made that way by attentive, caring owners.

Equally important when working with the therapy dog is the third motivator, *petting*.

It's not instinctive for a dog to enjoy being touched. Its normal reaction is defensive, until it has learned (in a deep, emotional way) to trust. This response must be conditioned through consistent touch that the dog finds pleasant, and it is the handler's responsibility to keep up this conditioning throughout the career of the therapy dog.

A therapy dog will be petted a great deal by gentle, considerate people. It will also be touched inappropriately at times. It's up to the handler to compensate for the inappropriate touch with good touch, to keep the dog tolerant. Make sure that pleasant touches always outnumber unpleasant touches by at least ten to one. Look at the context of the touches, too. For example, if a man mistreats or frightens the dog, a large number of pleasant experiences with men need to be arranged to prevent the dog from forming the opinion that men are bad.

Petting can also be used as a strong motivator for your dog. I used to let Saint go back to the tracklayer (who, after laying the track, follows handler and dog in case guidance is needed) for petting as a reward at the end of a successful scent track. Petting from someone he didn't see every day was a reward for Saint. Building in a therapy dog a deep enjoyment of being petted—by you and by others—will be a great asset in your work.

A puppy that's deprived of human contact may never be fully at ease with people. This is a critical period for socialization. An unsocialized dog can sometimes be reclaimed, but it's a long process. There is some evidence that the chief means of making up this lost time is through play, which is the fourth motivator in working your dog.

Like people, dogs use play to learn and to form and maintain relationships. The ability to play easily with a human is not found in all dogs. Some are not playful by nature, and others never learn because their owners don't know how to play with them. The more games you teach your dog, the more tools you'll have for communicating with the dog, training it, conditioning it to handling and exercising it. We'll talk more about play later in this chapter.

5.2. TEACHING THE DOG TO REMAIN STILL

One of the first things you can teach your dog through conditioning to handling is to remain still. This comes before any training to Stay on command. If the dog can't learn to remain still, it certainly can't learn a formal Stay. The dog that has the most trouble being still—trying to squirm free when held, perhaps banging its head back and forth and kicking with all four legs when held on its back—is the dog that most needs to be handled to learn to do so. This conditioning will also aid in visits to the veterinarian and during emergencies when the dog must stop struggling in order for anyone to be able to help it. The Stay command is basic to all dog training, without it you can't teach a dog much of anything.

I've had some dramatic experiences when the dog's relaxation to my touch saved the day. One such experience was when young Saint tried to jump over a wire crate and got caught, screaming and hanging from one alarmingly bent leg. I was able to lift him clear and carry him to the bed to calm him down and let me check him. Within a minute or two, he declared himself uninjured.

Another crisis came when Saint, playing the silly game of leading Star around by her buckle collar, got his head stuck. She thought he was refusing to let her go, and panicked. The ground was slick with ice, and it took me a few minutes to get to them. Star was growling and flailing, dragging Saint with her, and because it was dark out, I had to feel for the problem with my hands. If I'd had any doubts about my dogs, I might have hesitated to put my hands into such a fray. Yet when I touched them, it was awesome to feel both dogs instantly relax. I freed Saint quickly, and the relieved dogs soon seemed to forget all about it. This does not mean that dogs should go without identification collars; it was a freak accident, however, in this case, the dogs were in trouble.

These dogs didn't settle to my touch just because they loved me. Your dog can love you with all its heart and still react badly to your touch. They didn't respond because I had obedience trained them, either. Dogs can be obedience trained with virtually no conditioning to positive touch.

Saint and Star relaxed instantly to my hands because of years of connecting that touch with love and safety. Even when these hands discipline a dog, they do it with fairness and without causing the dog pain or injury. (Disipline should often be startling, but never painful.) If you're consistent about this with your dog, and if you spend the necessary regular time with it, you can have a dog that responds to touch in ways that will improve both your lives.

Remember that conditioning to handling isn't the time to give corrections. Before a dog is ready to learn any new command, it must develop the ability to do the thing you will later command it to do.

Some dogs can't be petted in obedience class as a means of reward because they aren't accustomed to it. Such dogs become overexcited when petted, and then must be corrected to bring them back under control. This problem results from owners not spending enough time petting their dogs. Make sure your dog regularly gets

Grooming helps condition a dog to handling. The white sheet catches loose hairs and helps detect the presence of external parasites.

Saint loves his daily rubdown.

enough petting so that it will not become overexcited when petted. This is essential to therapy dog work. Besides this, dogs have a basic need for touch. Dogs deprived of petting and attention often learn to misbehave because they are so starved for attention that even punishment is better than nothing.

Eventually your dog will become conditioned to the degree that your touch can reach through panic, if you can keep your head in a crisis. When frightening or painful things happen to your dog, they should always be accidents, and the dog needs to think of you as its rescuer. Even at the veterinarian's office, pain is never intentional, and the dog senses that—when it has the right foundation from you.

If you condition the dog properly, it will come to you, look to you, listen to you and respond to your touch in a true emergency. If you induce panic deliberately in your dog, especially repeatedly, the dog will learn to avoid you in times of stress. Also, don't try to trick your dog into thinking someone else caused the pain or fear, or that it was an accident when in fact you set it up. Don't use terrorist tactics in dog training. ***Be the one your dog can always trust.***

When conditioning the dog to remain still, you will touch the dog throughout. Whatever contact induces your dog to stop moving is good: scratch the inside of the thigh (that worked for Saint), rub the tummy or chest, scratch behind the ears, encircle the dog with your arms or hold it on your lap. If the dog starts to panic when you hold it still, find the point well short of panic that your dog can easily tolerate, and make that your starting point in conditioning.

You can lie down alongside the dog (convenient for owners who can safely allow their dogs on the bed). You can sit with your legs together, stretched in front of you, and lay the dog on its back on your legs, head or tail toward you—or first one way and then the other. You can stretch your legs out in a "V" and hold your dog in a sitting position in front of you, facing toward or away from you, or alternating directions. The more variations you do, the better.

Whatever the position, stroke the dog and talk to it in a pleasant voice as you hold it. If the dog finds it hard to remain still, lengthen the time gradually. Some dogs do this fairly naturally. It's a desirable trait to look for when testing a new dog, but you can probably teach it to the dog you have.

The dog is allowed to struggle lightly to ask you to release it. Don't release it immediately. Get it to settle again first, then release it. What you want to communicate is that your dog is allowed to ask to be released, but that you will decide when to release it. If you release instantly when it struggles, you're giving up control. Even worse is to hold on as the dog struggles more and more, and then finally let go. That teaches the dog to persist in fighting you, and to escalate the violence.

Be in a position to win. You want the dog to learn to be patient and to learn that you will let it free soon after it asks, when it's safe. You need this control for real-life situations, as well as for the right relationship with your dog.

You don't want to squelch your dog's willingness to communicate with you, so if there's no reason to keep the dog still, release it shortly after it asks you to and settles back down. Reward correct behavior by giving the dog what it wants, which in this case is to get free.

Have yourself and your dog in comfortable positions whenever you work on this skill. Make this experience pleasant for the dog—and for yourself.

5.3. PICKING THE DOG UP

Whether your dog is small or large, you would do well to learn (if you're strong enough) to pick the dog up whenever you wish. This improves your relationship with your dog, and gives you more options in unusual situations.

Picking up a dog of any size is not necessarily an easy skill. Many people lift even toy-sized dogs improperly. Always use both hands, no matter how small the dog. Improper lifting can cause the dog pain, or you may drop the dog and cause a terrible injury.

Angel taught me a lesson in picking up a small dog when I first got her. She was starved to two-thirds of her normal weight, and anything but perfect handling hurt, at which time she would emit a piercing scream. I learned to have her put her front feet up on my hand as I started to lift her, and in this way we worked together.

You need not train the therapy dog to be picked up by just anyone; in fact, I recommend that you do not allow the staff or other people in facilities to pick up your dog. It's too easy for the dog, not knowing someone else's moves, to zig when it should zag and get hurt. This not only risks injury, it can also ruin the dog's trust in you, in the visitation situation and in strangers.

If it's too late to stop someone from picking up your dog by

Every therapy dog handler should know the proper way to lift and carry a dog. In a small number of instances it will not be possible to lift a dog at all, but being able to do so enhances the bond of trust between dog and handler.

Always lift your therapy dog with both hands. Even small dogs should be treated in this fashion as serious injury can occur if a dog being lifted or carried is not handled securely.

Safe and happy in Bill's arms, Angel is securely supported across her chest and from beneath. In this position she is unlikely to come to any harm.

the time you notice, don't grab or yell. Watch carefully, and be ready in a split second to distract the dog if the person starts to hurt it. Next time, be more careful.

How should you pick up your dog? Have your veterinarian show you, if you aren't absolutely sure. In general, support the dog's weight securely on bones it uses to hold its weight when it stands, sits or lies down on its own. The dog will learn to help you by tensing the right muscles as you lift. If your dog is too large or heavy for you to securely lift, forget this exercise.

5.4. PLAYING GAMES WITH YOUR DOG

Okay, we have a dog that enjoys petting, holds still as we maintain physical contact and lets us pick it up, if we're strong enough. Now we'll use games to teach the dog more about how nice it is to be touched!

Since therapy dogs interact with people, and since play is a major way dogs interact with others, teaching these dogs to play with humans is important, although dogs that aren't playful can still make good therapy dogs. There are also some dogs who only play games that don't fit into therapeutic interaction. It's still well worth the time to play these games with your dog at home, because they strengthen your relationship with your dog, and aid both conditioning to handling and training for control. Play can be used to build in your dog the drives to work, to follow through on a task and to try to please you.

As you progress in training, you will use play to help your dog learn to obey a command when it isn't in an alert, ready-to-work mode. This is an essential control skill for a therapy dog, because often the dog will be interacting with other people when given commands. Start by playing games at home and using them between control exercises, when no one else is around to be inconvenienced or endangered if the dog is slow to come back to work.

Gradually you can develop in your dog the ability to play when you want to play, to work when you want to work and to shift gears from one to the other smoothly, at your wish. But don't expect this at the beginning. If you do, you'll dampen the dog's enjoyment of play and damage one of your strongest motivators for training.

What games can you play with your dog? You and your dog

will develop many of your own—that's the joy of play. Keep in mind behavior you wish to encourage in your dog, and behavior you wish to discourage. Maintain the ability to stop the game at any point.

Often the best correction for a dog getting too rowdy in play is for you to simply refuse to play anymore. It's not a dominant act, and therefore will work with a puppy that isn't yet trained, a dog you haven't had long or a dog that may not totally accept you as leader yet. This is how one dog treats another dog that gets too rough in play. It's negative feedback that will often teach the dog to play more appropriately in future.

Stop the game for perhaps fifteen minutes, long enough for an overstimulated dog to calm down. If you restart the game and the dog again misbehaves, stop immediately. On the second or third repetition of this, the dog begins to understand what it's doing wrong: repetition is an important learning tool. Also, stop the game whenever the dog's teeth touch you in play. Don't let the dog think it's okay to put its teeth on people.

With all games, play with your dog when you feel like it. Don't give the dog control of when you play, or for how long. You can allow your dog to solicit play, and you can play if you want to in response to the dog's request—this helps the dog learn to communicate with you. But if you're not in the mood, refuse.

Most dog trainers prefer to work with a dog that cares about pleasing the trainer. This is an extremely desirable, but not essential, trait in a therapy dog. Many dogs simply haven't been conditioned properly to develop this trait. Play can help, offering many ways to enhance your dog's intelligence and ability.

5.5. RETRIEVING

Retrieving is the healthiest and most popular game people play with dogs. It's best to teach retrieving in play before you start formal work to make it a command. The first rule is to never punish your dog when you take anything out of its mouth or when it brings something to you.

When your dog has something in its mouth you don't want it to have, give it something nice in return for giving you that object. For this purpose I keep lots of dog toys around, and make the replacement toy exciting by playing with the dog and it for a moment before letting the dog have the toy all to itself. This teaches the dog to give things up without resentment. If the dog has a particularly harmful object, you can spank and scold *the object* (*not* the dog) before giving the dog a replacement toy. This will discourage the dog from touching that object in the future without harming the dog's working ability.

A simple tactic used to shape play-retrieving is not to throw a toy for the dog again unless the dog brings the first back to you. Try using a tennis ball. It's relatively resistant to chewing and unlikely to break furniture or cause an injury.

When your dog brings something to you—or you have to take something out of its mouth—don't pull the object out. This encourages the dog to bite harder and resist you. Some dogs will easily give the object up if you place your hand on the object with no pressure. Another tactic is to grasp the dog's collar with one hand while you reach for the object with the other. Sometimes just holding the collar is enough of a reminder to the dog of who is in charge. If you need to do more, take your hand and grasp the dog's upper jaw, firmly but gently. With your other hand, remove the object from the dog's mouth. Don't let it be a fight between you and the dog. Just take control.

Use caution if you decide to force-train your therapy dog to retrieve. In this training, the dog is subjected to pain such as having its ear pinched to get it to open its mouth, which may be accompanied by a scream from the dog. When done with precise timing by a skilled trainer, this need not be cruel. However, you wouldn't want your therapy dog to react to an accidental painful touch from a person on a visit by opening its mouth, screaming and trying to grab at something to stop the pain. This could become a reflex if the trainer isn't careful.

The handler who wishes to train a therapy dog to retrieve reliably on command should shop carefully for the right method for that dog. The retrieving instinct is, however, one that puppies and dogs can be tested for. If your dog has a strong retrieving instinct and you're diligent and patient, you can probably develop a reliable retrieve with a minimum of force. If, when you throw an object, your dog runs out, picks it up and carries it—whether to you or off to play—it's promising.

Take It and Hold It can be taught as gentle, stationary exercises that you begin after the dog has begun retrieving in play (brings the object back to you after you throw it, most of the time). Use a

Saint's education as a therapy dog involved a great deal of gentle conditioning and handling. As a result, this kind-hearted fellow is not upset by an intense examination of his left ear.

standard wooden or plastic dumbbell such as those used in obedience training. Make sure the dog can comfortably hold it, and doesn't get poked in the eye when it holds the dumbbell by the bit. Sometimes it takes a little experimenting to find a dumbbell that fits the dog properly, but this is time well spent.

Don't force the Take It; just gently place the dumbbell into the dog's mouth. It's important for a therapy dog handler to be able to confidently handle the dog's mouth. If necessary, open the mouth by grasping the upper jaw. Then say "Hold it," and support the dog's chin. Dogs tend to drop the chin before dropping the object, so hold the chin up.

After the dog gets used to this, start taking your supporting hand away. Before putting the dumbbell in, offer it to the dog, saying "Take it." If the dog takes the dumbbell without your help, give liberal praise—this is an excellent sign. Build up time on the Hold It gradually, counting the seconds. Decide in advance that it will be two seconds this time, or five seconds, or whatever, and help the dog do it that long before you release—don't just release when you see the dog about to quit.

If the dog drops the dumbbell while on the Hold It command, you can correct it with a gentle but abrupt two-fingered slap under the chin, being careful not to make the teeth bite the tongue.

When you take the dumbbell out of the dog's mouth, use the word you want for your command to release the object. Some say "Out," others say "Give." I occasionally say "Thank you!" This command can also be used when you take a forbidden object from your dog around the house.

Once the dog holds the dumbbell reliably when seated, begin having the dog stand up and walk with it. Gradually add distance. The dog should be on leash.

When the dog is steady, you can put your retrieve together, combining play, the dog's basic drives, your careful conditioning and the command control you've taught your dog. Do the slap correction on Hold It no more than three times in any practice session, and not more than about a dozen times over the whole training process. Coming from under the chin, this correction is not threatening to the dog. If you have to do it too many times, you're trying to get the dog to progress too fast. Retrieving training is best done over a long period of time. A year is not unusual.

Competitive obedience trials and hunting work may require a more precise retrieve, trained with more force. You must be the

Until your dog will take the dumbbell willingly, *gently* place it into the dog's mouth on the command "Take it." Like most dogs, Star loves her dumbbell and enjoys the exercise.

"Hold it." Bill supports Star's chin.

judge of how your dog is treated and how you wish to live and work with the dog.

Extended retrieving games, in which you hide something from the dog and the dog seeks it out, give you the opportunity to observe your dog's working style and to encourage the dog to develop persistence when working on a task. Make it a little challenging, but not so hard that the dog gives up. It's fine to use food as the object, especially at first.

Here are safety hints for using retrieving on therapy dog visits:

1. Do retrieving games only with a clear area in which the dog may move. Unless the dog is on a long line or a retracting leash under your control, avoid these games in unfenced areas, due to unpredictable throws.

2. Keep the leash on for retrieving games in which others throw the object for the dog. Watch the ball until you can see that the dog has a clear path to it before you release. Use the leash to stop the dog from running into people or snapping at the ball near anyone. This requires considerable handling experience and skill with the leash.

3. Have the dog bring you the object for you to pass to the next person. This way people can take turns, which is socially stimulating. The dog would not understand to take it to the next person; or not to, in the case of an unruly child who needs to miss a turn. This also prevents the dog's teeth from getting near anyone's hand. Instead, you handle the dog's mouth.

4. Use a tennis ball or other soft object. If a wild throw hits the dog or a person, a tennis ball is unlikely to cause harm.

This method of handling a dog when it retrieves for other people is more work for the handler, but it's safe. Some dogs are almost dainty when retrieving around people and you may not need all the precautions. However, even these dogs may get more vigorous as they gain experience, so observe your dog and add extra control when required.

If you have several dogs, avoid excessive competition among them in this or any game. Provide plenty of objects for them all to retrieve or seek. Throw toys in different directions, and use each dog's name to cue it when that throw is for that dog. Never throw one toy for multiple dogs to chase—that's asking for disaster.

If you can't get your dogs to cooperate, work them separately.

"No! Hold it!" The correction for dropping the dumbbell is a gentle, but abrupt reprimand, nothing stronger.

"Give," "Out," or "Thank You."

"Hold it," while walking. Keep the dog on lead, but don't use a "Heel" command.

Star learned to pick up the dumbbell as an extension of her natural retrieving instinct, strengthened by play over an extended period.

A happily-working retriever.

With patience, you may get them to work together eventually. This is most convenient, as it lets you play impromptu games with the dogs without first having to separate them. If you can work and play with them in each other's presence, they will stimulate each other to learn.

Anything your dog does that you like can become the basis of a game. Many of the benefits of play come from the fact that it's spontaneous. Keep in mind the commands you want your dog to learn and how you want the dog to behave with people. Use play to help achieve your goals.

5.6. TO TUG OR NOT TO TUG?

One game that you may not want to play with your dog is tug-of-war. Some trainers say not to do this with any dog, because it's too dangerous, but sometimes it's a matter of learning to do it properly.

I enjoy owning submissive dogs, and have no doubt that I must be their leader, for their own good. But some dogs, however, are naturally dominant, and unless the owner is an expert, such a dog should not be taught tug-of-war. It pits the dog's strength against the owner's, and can lead to other confrontations. You don't want to fight with your dog.

A child has no hope of dominance with many dogs, and therefore should be discouraged from playing tug-of-war. It's not worth the risk.

Another problem is when a dog loves tug-of-war so much that it wants to play it all the time. This game should have only a minor role in your interaction with your dog. Don't play it too often, or for too long a time. You should find that you do it less and less, as you and your dog find more interesting things to do together. If this isn't happening, take a close look at your tug-of-war games to make sure you aren't risking a dangerous confrontation. This is important because, as dogs age, their urge to become dominant increases. What was okay with a young dog may not be okay with the same dog at age two, four, six or older. The aging dog is also more easily injured and may not heal well regardless of how accidental injury comes about.

When playing, don't pull your dog's neck from side to side even if the dog wants to. Make your pulls straight. The dog likes little jerks, but jerk lightly toward yourself and let the dog jerk back. Don't tolerate injury to yourself, either. If the dog's teeth touch you, stop the game. If the dog is clearly submissive to you, give a loud "yipe" when you feel the teeth, so the dog knows it hurt you. Even if it doesn't hurt that much, the dog needs this feedback—the same feedback it would get from another dog. Stop the game for fifteen minutes—or for the day, if you don't want to play anymore.

If you find your dog is too submissive, you can build its confidence by letting it "win" at tug-of-war, but not every time. If you take on the responsibility of playing this game, you must also accept the responsibility of staying in control. That means making sure the dog will give up the article to you any time you say, no matter how excited it is.

After a submissive dog gives you the object on command, you can give it back to the dog. You may want to say "Give," or whatever your "Out" command on the retrieve is to be, to reinforce your retrieving work. If the object is something your dog can't safely keep, give the dog another toy in its place.

If you find that you can't get the dog to surrender the article on your command, all tug-of-war games with that dog must stop. Not only is the game dangerous with such a dog, but you will make the dog feel more dominant and increase the risk of someone getting bitten.

Animating the object in order to make it more desirable and to "turn the dog on" is the true purpose of tug-of-war in dog training. It can help teach your dog that it must give things up to you when you say so, and can reinforce your control over your dog. Like many tools in dog training, it's powerful when you do it right, harmful when you do it wrong. It should not be a real battle between human and dog. If it ever becomes that, stop.

Tug-of-war should not be used on therapy dog visits. It makes the dog look "tough," which is not the public image you want to convey. It encourages the dog to get rowdy and perhaps even domineering—both wrong attitudes for a therapy setting. Also, it can encourage the people watching to try to get the dog to play tug-of-war with them, which could be dangerous.

5.7. INHIBITING THE BITE

Another important aspect of conditioning the therapy dog to handling is inhibiting the tendency to bite. Most families would prefer their dogs to have this conditioning, too. Unfortunately, many dog owners condition their dogs incorrectly regarding the use of its teeth.

If a puppy stays in its litter long enough, or has normal relationships with other dogs, it will learn, from the other dogs, not to bite too hard. Once a dog knows how to inhibit the bite with other dogs, however, it must learn a new standard for people. Dog skin is much thicker and stronger than human skin. Tooth pressure that wouldn't even cause discomfort for another dog can tear right through human skin. Your dog can't know this unless you teach it.

Whenever a dog's tooth touches your hand, let your hand go limp. You could hurt yourself by yanking the hand away and scraping it on a tooth. Jerking could also stimulate the dog to grab or hold your hand with its teeth. As you and your dog progress in conditioning together, you may want to introduce some jerking in order to condition the dog not to reflexively respond by grabbing, in case this happens on a therapy dog visit. Approach this gradually and carefully.

In some cases rough corrections for putting teeth on human skin are warranted. Such corrections could include a slap to the muzzle (a glancing slap, not a punch), a lightning-fast collar correction if the dog is on leash or if your hand is in the dog's mouth, pushing it farther in to gag the dog. However, these may be too rough for a submissive dog that just doesn't know any better. Try the ''yipe,'' and shun the dog for a few minutes. Dogs use this form of feedback with each other, so your dog would understand.

None of the techniques mentioned here are for the dog that genuinely intends to bite you. If this is the case with your dog, or if you have any fear of your dog, get the help of a professional before it's too late. This professional will need to interact with both your dog and your family in order to diagnose and solve the problem.

How my three dogs learned to inhibit the bite exemplifies some situations that can be handled at home.

The easiest was Angel. She was already strongly inhibited against biting humans at the age of eighteen months when I adopted her. She's small and white, leading other dogs to treat her gently. White, which often appears on the bellies of dogs, is a flag of submission in the canine world. Angel doesn't even have to roll over to get many dogs to view her as nonthreatening. If she needs to do more than just be white, she has a traffic-stopping scream, which she has found adequate for expressing any objection. Angel also has a complete repertoire of canine language, and can hit one shoulder on the ground in a flash, to turn the other dog off. It's fascinating to watch. The same language works for her with people, on whom she never puts her teeth.

Saint, half Labrador and half German shepherd, is a tender-mouthed retriever, an instinct selectively bred into some dogs so they won't damage game when retrieving for a hunter. Saint only bites down on food or things with which he's playing. As soon as he feels a hand in his mouth, he pulls his teeth away from it. He's black with erect ears, and adept at canine language. With other dogs, Saint spends most of his time expressing to them that they needn't be afraid of his big, black self. He will lie down, turn his head sideways, pull his lips over his teeth to hide them, lower his ears, run away to encourage the other dog to chase him, and otherwise communicate his goodwill.

When we got Saint from the city animal shelter at a rowdy nine months of age, his biggest problem was swinging his open mouth around and accidentally bumping us with his teeth. Our "yiping" solved this problem. He would rather die than hurt us.

A related problem came with his mania for retrieving. He liked to play tug-of-war, too, but for him that was just an appetizer to retrieving. In play, he would carelessly bump our hands with his teeth.

I taught Saint a special command called Close Your Mouth. I did this by encircling his muzzle with one hand and then holding it shut for about fifteen seconds. If you try this, make sure you don't pinch the dog's lip or tongue against its teeth. Making this correction painful for the dog could make it dangerous for you. Hold the dog just beyond the time it protests and then settles back down. Don't release the dog when it's struggling, but don't hold it for five minutes, either. Then, while holding the muzzle, say "Close your mouth." This restraint is slightly unpleasant for the dog. Saint likes to avoid it whenever he can. Therefore he quickly learned to respond to the command or to my signal of forming my right hand into a backwards "C" shape. The same command and signal work to tell a dog to stop barking, and also helps therapy dog handlers when they practice handling their dog's mouth.

This command actually serves as a mild threat, telling Saint that if he doesn't shut his mouth, I will do it for him. Remember, it's a restraint, not a violent or painful correction. When I need to add more impact to it, I go nose-to-nose with Saint as I hold his mouth, glare him in the eye and speak to him firmly (but often quietly) about his behavior. I don't yank his neck around or make him bite his tongue or lips. The quiet voice is a good technique with dogs, for just as with noisy children, they have to get quiet to hear you.

My third dog, Star, a Belgian Tervuren, presented a more complicated situation. She's extremely submissive, active, obedient and loving, yet she is of a herding breed that uses gentle nipping and holding to control sheep. Star frequently nips and grips both of my other dogs. They don't mind it at all, and it does them no harm.

But of course Star can't be allowed to nip and grip people. Teaching her not to do so was complicated by the fact that she knew she wasn't hurting me, so didn't believe my "yipe." And it was a strong instinct; she had an enormous drive to interact with me by using her teeth in this way.

She easily learned the Close Your Mouth, but didn't quickly stop touching me with her teeth as Saint had. I had to keep telling her. One helpful correction was to hold her upper jaw for fifteen seconds with my hand whenever she mouthed me, the idea being that if she put her mouth on me, I'd take it away for a while. It helped without traumatizing her, but it wasn't enough.

With an aggressive dog a more severe correction might have been in order, but tough corrections don't work well with submissive dogs. They get so upset they can't think, and then all they learn is not to trust you. Therefore, I decided to try an approach that often works when dealing with an undesirable instinct: redirect the dog's behavior. You should avoid correcting a dog harshly for something it has a strong instinct to do, unless you're willing to destroy that behavior in the dog completely, and risk damaging its working ability. Instead, teach the dog to do something different whenever the problematic instinct is stimulated inappropriately.

I taught Star a word for licking. Now, whenever I see that she wants to put her teeth on me, I tell her to "kiss" instead. She gets to respond to what her herding-dog nature craves, and I get what I want.

These examples illustrate only a few possible situations. If you get your dog as a puppy, you will need to go through the puppy stage of inhibiting the bite, too. A puppy or dog that learns it's okay

Teaching the correction "Close your mouth" *or* "No more barking"...

...and the signal.

to bite people will develop serious problems. It is necessary to find a way to deal with this because, in the long run, your dog's life may be at stake, and of course there is no way that a dog who regularly bites people can work as a therapy dog.

5.8. TEASING

Teasing is often involved in play with dogs. As long as the dog is having fun, it will be in the ideal mental state to learn, and it won't be especially sensitive to pain. Playful, thoughtful teasing can increase a dog's tolerance for handling and improve both your control over the dog and the dog's self-control. If at any time in a game the dog stops having fun, then the game has gone too far.

Teasing must never become abusive to the dog, nor to the person teasing. In play, the dog can learn what hurts people and what doesn't, how to move around so as not to trip or injure people and other lessons that can help a therapy dog. Teasing is a wilder form of play. Work up to it gradually, and use good judgment.

Teach children not to tease dogs—and that includes tug-of-war. Children cannot be expected to know what is appropriate teasing and what is not. They can get hurt, and they can ruin good dogs.

Teasing is used to train protection and guard dogs. You don't want your therapy dog made dangerously and inappropriately aggressive by teasing. This can happen accidentally when a dog is kept chained outdoors. People and other animals pass by, just out of reach, and the dog may want more and more to get at them. Then one day something goes wrong with the chain or the collar, or someone resembling somebody who's been teasing the dog comes within reach, and a protection drive that's been teased gets acted on. For the same reason, you must make sure no one teases your dog over the backyard fence.

One of the most valuable uses of teasing—as long as you can maintain control—is getting the dog really worked up and then helping it to exercise self-control. At this point you can also work on inhibiting the bite. When the dog wants to put its teeth on you, show it what to do instead. You should, of course, never do this with a dog you don't know well.

Teasing should be fun for both you and the dog, should never be in danger of getting out of control and should never go on too long. Dogs get worked up as they play longer and longer. They get

Bill and Star demonstrate the correction for mouthing a person. The dog's mouth is held open gently in a "time out" for about fifteen seconds.

tired at the same time, and may miss and bite you by accident, or injure themselves. For the same reason, if dogs seem to be getting too wild playing with each other, make them take a break.

5.9. PHYSICAL DISCIPLINE

Sometimes it's proper to use physical discipline with a dog, though not nearly as often as people do it. This enters into conditioning to handling, whether by plan or by accident. Some dogs in obedience training, for example, learn to tolerate neck-jerk collar corrections. Other dogs become increasingly intolerant of such corrections. Dogs have different body sensitivities—what is comfortable for one dog may be abusive for another. A major problem, too, is correction given by a poor trainer. If the correction is poorly timed, unfair, or too violent, the stress on the dog is greatly increased.

Dogs need motivation in order to learn and to work (as do people), and corrections do not motivate. Corrections can stop some bad behavior patterns, but they don't create good ones. Whatever motivator you used to teach something—food, praise, petting or play—will need to be given often enough to keep the dog doing that behavior. How long would you work without any reward or thanks? You would lose heart—so does a dog.

Physical correction should only be used when the dog knows what it's supposed to do and rebelliously does the wrong thing, or when it's behaving dangerously. It should be used in the mildest form possible to stop the dog from misbehaving. Usually, this means using restraint. Violent corrections only seem to train a dog more quickly when in fact they usually create new problems. There are no shortcuts to good training.

Use your hands so often to caress the dog that an occasional correction with hands won't change the dog's belief that hands mean love. You are unlikely to harm the dog with a light slap (*never* a blow or punch) on the thickest part of the thigh. The slap should not cause the dog to cry out. If you must slap a small dog, use one or two fingers, not your whole hand. This slap should be no harder than what the dog would enjoy as hearty petting—it's the timing that communicates, not the force. When the dog obeys after a slap (which is the point of doing it), immediately pet the dog with the same hand and praise.

Another method of correction is to put your hand on the side of the dog's shoulder and push its front slightly sideways. This is a sign of your dominance. Do not use this gesture unless the issue of leadership has long been settled between you and your dog. Used with a dog that does not accept you as leader, it could get you bitten.

When the dog attempts to steal food or playfully nips you, you can use two fingers (one finger with a small dog) to slap down on the muzzle.

All corrections must be scaled to the size of the dog. Never give a physical correction when you are angry. If you must do something in anger, yell. When you are angry your reflexes are affected, and a proper physical correction to a dog demands flawless timing. A little humor doesn't hurt, either.

Always teach the dog what it should be doing in place of the action for which you're correcting. If you don't know what the dog should be doing instead, you're not ready to give a physical correction. You can destroy your dog's temperament and working ability through giving poor corrections, so never correct your dog until you fully understand the reason for its actions.

Some dogs shouldn't be corrected by anyone other than their owners. If you have such a dog, you have the responsibility and the right to insist that others not correct it. This includes obedience class. If another person, even an instructor, corrects your dog inappropriately (which can easily happen, since no one but you knows the dog really well), your dog's working ability may be ruined. You may be able to rehabilitate the dog through a long conditioning process, or you may not. No one has the right to do that to you and your dog.

An excellent method of correction for a therapy dog is to have it repeat an action it didn't perform properly. If necessary, give the dog more help the second time. When using this technique of boring repetition as a correction, let the dog stop after it does the action right. Remember to give generous praise.

A good physical correction is to set up the situation so that, if the dog disobeys, it will meet with some undesirable consequence. One example is to turn and go the other way if your dog is pulling on the leash. Another is to walk near a post when the dog is not staying close enough to you on an on-leash walk. The dog will wind up on the wrong side of the post and see for itself why it needs to pay attention. These corrections need not be done violently.

You can also set things up so that if the dog moves when it shouldn't, something will fall over. Of course it shouldn't be anything that could hurt the dog. Another situational correction is to tie

Here Bill uses body language to apply a correction. Star understands and apologizes.

the dog that tends to break a Stay to something behind, with slack in the line. It will start to leave and think it's going to make it, then hit the end of the line. I prefer tying the dog to something, rather than having another person hold the line.

Your body language is an excellent way to correct your dog, because dogs live in a world of body language. You can glare at your dog, shake your finger, stamp your foot, etc. Be sure to give lots of positive body language when the dog behaves correctly. If you're always negative, the dog may learn to ignore you.

The therapy dog needs at least ten times as much reward as it gets correction, preferably much more. It needs this same ten-to-one (or greater) proportion of positive touch over negative touch if it's to develop and maintain the proper response to being touched. Minimize the number of corrections you give by teaching the dog what to do, rather than correcting it. Then the dog gets praised, and your problem gets solved. This approach creates a more confident dog and your training will take the minimum amount of time, since you won't waste time rehabilitating the dog for problems created by excessive corrections.

5.10. A CUDDLE A DAY . . .

Find time to cuddle your dog every day. We all get busy, and it's easy to neglect this. If you groom your dog every day (which has wonderful benefits, too), that can be a time for hugging and petting, before or after grooming. When you wake up in the morning, go to bed at night or watch television, you can spend time cuddling your dog.

Lots of people will pet your dog on therapy dog visits, and many will do it incorrectly. To offset this, the therapy dog needs plenty of good petting from friendly strangers. But most of all, your dog needs it from you. Your petting is the gold standard for your dog. No matter what a "love everybody" dog it is, there is no substitute for your love.

Dog owners with multiple dogs often complain that they can't pet or praise one dog without another getting jealous. My dogs know I won't tolerate competition near me. It's too dangerous for dogs to flash out at each other, even in otherwise-acceptable dog discussions, when right next to a human. If you live intimately with a group of dogs, you know that the dominant dog flashes lightning fast at the submissive one, and the submissive one knows just how and when to dodge that move, as if they were dancing. These interactions are sometimes playful, sometimes symbolic. Even though my dogs don't fight with each other, if they played too near a person, that person could easily get in the way and be bitten or knocked down, when that wasn't at all what the dogs intended.

Dogs must learn to distance this interaction from people, a control especially essential for your therapy dog, because it's unsafe for dogs to fight or play with each other on therapy dog visits. Yet in order to maintain good social abilities, dogs benefit from expressing these normal dog-to-dog behaviors at appropriate times.

One way to teach multiple dogs to interact at a safe distance from people is to banish them from your immediate presence whenever they roughhouse too near you. If they're on the bed with you, it's "Off the bed!" Send them all away. Don't attempt to determine who did what.

When you praise or pet one dog and another comes up wanting to join in, try to include both dogs. This greatly reduces competition for your attention and seems to build a sort of team spirit. They learn that if one of them does well, they can all have praise and petting. Knowing this, they often become less needy and more content to wait for your attention. Also be careful not to give a new dog or a submissive dog so much attention that it arouses jealousy in the dog you have had longer or the more dominant dog in the pack. When playing, dogs tend to get along better if they have room to run and act out body language. Violence is more likely to occur in close quarters.

After the dogs learn to cooperate for cuddling, you may find that you can give a loving look or word to one dog across the room while holding another, making both happy. You may also find that they seem pleased when they see you pet the other dogs.

It's essential to spend plenty of private time with each dog, because the only way you can control a pack of dogs together is to have complete control over each individually.

During these private daily sessions, you can condition your therapy dog to handle many necessary aspects of interaction with people. One of these is having people in its face.

Children are often bitten because they put their faces next to dogs' faces. Since this can be dangerous, you must do the conditioning cautiously. Wait until you know the dog and have control over it before starting.

There cannot be too much personal interaction between a therapy dog and the members of its human family. Even after a demanding training session, there's still room in the schedule for Bill and Star to get close.

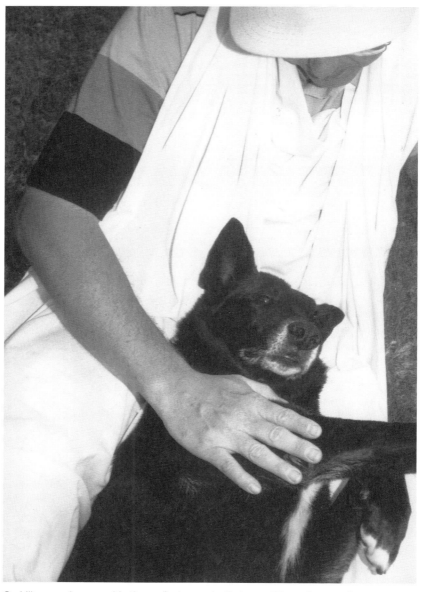

Cuddling sessions provide the perfect opportunity to condition a therapy dog to respond properly to people close to its face.

When you first put your face next to the dog's face—or any time you do it suddenly—the dog may forget who you are and treat you as it would treat another dog. They gnaw and snap and do a lot of things with each other that humans can't endure. A dog can injure a person's face with the exact same motion and pressure that another dog would enjoy. Bites to the face can be the most serious dog bites to humans. Cuddling time is a natural time for you to teach your therapy dog how to behave around people's faces.

I've learned through hard knocks that when a dog rises the head leads, and can pack a wallop! That's how dogs move, and until the dog gets used to moving around people, the impact can accidentally give a split lip or other injury. An easy way to prevent this is to keep your hand on the top of the dog's head or the back of its neck. This will remind the dog that you're there. You can hold the dog's head steady as it rises.

Many people in facilities can't control their movements. Your dog will encounter people who don't know how to move around a dog, or who fear dogs and telegraph this through their movements. By playing with your dog at cuddling time, you can get it used to all sorts of human movements. End each disturbing movement with something the dog likes, such as tummy rubbing.

In all conditioning of your dog to handling, remember your goal of teaching the dog to read people and to interact with them. Start by using good "dog language" to relate to your dog, then gradually accustom the dog to typical human language and behavior. Work your way up to hugging the dog, kissing the dog on its face and touching the dog while it's eating. If other people are ever to be able to do these things safely with your dog, you must do them first, and regularly. These must not be challenges for dominance between person and dog. They must be easy, give-and-take communications, and this takes time.

The time you spend regularly cuddling your therapy dog is even more important than training time. Through cuddling, you bond the dog to yourself. Training also creates bonds, but sometimes mistakes are made in training and the dog is pushed too hard. Cuddling time can undo this damage. I find that spending regular time cuddling my dogs actually makes them more obedient.

Petting a dog lowers a human's blood pressure, and it even eases the pain of my arthritis. A cuddle a day is good medicine!

Many of the skills dogs learn in obedience training are similar to those required in therapy dog applications. While many of the advances in therapy dog training came through the activities of those who train competitive obedience trial dogs, it is important to recognize the differences as well as the similarities in the two fields.

6

Basic Control

MUCH OF THE PROGRESS IN THERAPY DOG
work has come through trainers who participate in the sport of obedience competition. Clarifying the differences between competition training and therapy dog training can make this relationship smoother and more productive. Obedience competition is a sport. Training and handling for therapy dog visits is neither a sport nor is it competitive. Typically, a potential therapy dog will be neither defiant nor tough. Yet some of the best competitive obedience dogs are both, as are a large percentage of dogs brought to instructors for civilizing. Many dog-training techniques are derived from the training of tough and dominant dogs for police and military work. This means the curriculum can be wrong for your therapy dog.

6.1. FINDING HELP

In training your dog, the first thing to do is decide on your goals. You'll need to do this from time to time throughout your life with dogs. For now your goal is to work with therapy dogs.

Another area goal setting enters into is family life. Most dogs can live as companion animals and also do a job outside the home. Some people will place the dog's job priorities over the home priorities. I think it works better to put home priorities first. Most people live with their dogs at home much more than they work with them. Therefore, goals include the training your dog needs to function well with your lifestyle.

Before you can get good behavior from your dog, you must decide what behavior you want. Training your dog to fit your needs takes time and makes it especially important to have goals. Otherwise, that same time will pass, and your dog will be no better behaved!

Your goals will change as you learn. For example, few people who enroll in a training class for the first time plan to show their dogs in obedience competition. A small percentage of them get "hooked" and go on to that goal. In the process, they usually get a wonderful education in dog handling, which alone would make the time spent worthwhile.

Another important reason to have goals is that without them you may never feel you've succeeded. Goals let you say, "I set out to do that, and I did it!" This sense of achievement is emotionally healthy for you, and you'll give your dog extra love and attention for helping you—which is great for the dog. Have short-term and small goals as well as long-term and large goals, so you can celebrate often.

Once you have goals in mind, you're prepared to start seeking help with training, and these goals will help you select an instructor, too. If you want to train your dog as a therapy dog, you aren't looking for someone to train your dog for you. You'll need to work to thoroughly understand and share a close friendship with your dog. You'll need to develop the skill to handle that dog in all situations, and you'll need to maintain that dog's training yourself as you work with it for the rest of its life. Therefore, you're seeking an instructor to teach *you*. You will teach the dog, with the instructor's help. The training should help prepare you to choose and train other dogs yourself in the future. It's like the old idea that it's better to teach people to fish than to give them fish today and leave them to get hungry again tomorrow.

A private trainer can provide a fine alternative to obedience class. If your dog has a problem interacting with other dogs, you should train with a private instructor first, and enter a class only with that person's help and advice. If your dog is a sweetheart with other dogs, it can go to fun matches, classes, and other dog events under the guidance of a private instructor. This individual help—if the instructor is the right one for you—may well increase your chances of success. Keep in mind that evaluating the competence of an instructor is often difficult for a beginning dog trainer. Choose an instructor carefully, and be sure to discuss your goals with this person.

Two other options are attending seminars and reading books. Seminars are short-term, one-shot deals, and the person in charge isn't interacting fully with, nor does this person know, you or your dog. This can lead to inappropriate training, which can ruin your dog. Seminars are great, however, if you think things through before incorporating new ideas into the way you treat your dog. You should attend at least three seminars before making any major change.

The same goes for books. Few books will be 100 percent right for your situation, but there are hundreds of dog books. You can surely find three that will lead you through the thinking process to a plan that will work for you and your dog.

When armed with your goals, you're ready to evaluate an obedience class, private trainer, seminar or book to decide if it's right for you. Here are some questions to think about in choosing the help you'll use:

1. What kind of dogs has this trainer (or writer) owned? This is more important than the dogs taught in classes, because instructors don't get to know class dogs as well. A trainer's philosophy and the techniques he or she uses will be based more on the type of dogs he or she has owned than on any other factor.

   You need someone who owns the same general type of dog you do. It doesn't have to be the same breed. Important similarities can be grouped: guard dogs, sled dogs, herding dogs, terriers, large dogs, small dogs, shy dogs, aggressive dogs, sensitive dogs, responsive dogs, retrievers, dogs bred to do the same type of work as your breed and other factors you consider important to understanding your dog. Look for someone who understands—and loves—your kind of dog.

2. Has this trainer (writer) participated in the work you plan to do with your dog? Is he or she still active in the work? Do you respect and admire the trainer's efforts in this field?

3. In observing this trainer (or reading his or her work), are you comfortable with the way dogs are treated? If not, walk away, close the book, take your dog home!

4. Can you communicate well with this instructor? If the instructor intimidates you, your goals may never be considered. You must remain in control of how your dog is treated.
5. What do other dog handlers whose opinions you respect think of this instructor? Dog people love to talk about dogs and training ideas. Don't be shy about calling, writing or approaching another trainer politely in public and asking for help. (Be cautious when approaching people at competitive dog events, however. They might rebuff you out of nervousness. Matches are usually more relaxed and a better place to meet people and ask questions.) Talking to other dog people can be your best means of finding the right instructor in your community to help you and your dog.

6.2. BASIC PRINCIPLES

Although you'll need to seek specific help with your dog, and although one book isn't enough to tell you how to train your dog, I don't feel this book would be complete without a description of the basic control exercises a therapy dog and handler need to know, and at least one gentle way to teach them to a dog. Be sure to tailor this advice to your dog.

Two important ideas are central to therapy dog training, and *initiative* is the first. The therapy dog should ideally be taught to think for itself and to share its thoughts with you. You'll have trouble with this concept if you don't believe dogs can think. Initiative is also called intelligent disobedience or responsibility, and is a factor in the training of many working dogs, including dogs that guide the blind, dogs that aid the deaf, police dogs, hunting dogs and others.

Whenever people depend on a dog's senses, which are more acute than human senses, the dog needs initiative. Sometimes the dog's senses will pick up information that tells it a human's command is wrong. If you want to take full advantage of your dog's abilities in therapy dog work, you need to develop the dog's initiative, while still keeping good control. It's a fascinating challenge.

The second basic principle is: *Never correct or punish your dog when it's in the act of being friendly.*

You may intend the punishment for some other misdeed, but if the dog is in the act of being friendly, correction at that moment

110

risks making the dog dislike people or lose the desire to interact with strangers.

This restriction also extends to when the dog is acting friendly toward another dog. This doesn't mean letting your dog bother others. Instead of punishing, restrain your dog. Hold the dog back, or pull it back without jerking. Redirect the dog's attention. Neither punish nor correct your dog at any time when that dog might experience the correction as a negative result of being friendly.

These two ideas are essential for training your dog to develop so that it can initiate communication with people and respond to them. Most dogs can be so much more than puppets; however, there are dogs that will not make responsible decisions if allowed to take initiative. Such dogs are not the best prospects for therapy dogs, but can be used with the right handlers. I won't name breeds, but some are usually trained fairly harshly and strictly to obey, never to make independent decisions. I suspect that there really are dogs that can't be trusted and that owning such dogs is why some trainers believe that no dog can be trusted. You need to determine what kind of dog you have.

The exercises that follow are not difficult to learn, if you practice regularly for several months, and practice properly. They can become a problem when you try to accomplish through severe corrections what you should have accomplished through practice. A dog treated in such an unfair manner can become traumatized about that exercise, and unreliable performing it. Rehabilitating the dog may well take longer than it would have taken to train properly in the first place, and will not be as much fun.

You may also want to introduce the basic exercises in a different order than presented here to suit your needs, or start them all at the same time, so your practice sessions are interesting for you and the dog. Sessions that are from five to twenty minutes long are right for most dogs. Some dogs can happily work longer than twenty minutes at a time, especially if practice of control exercises is interspersed with play. If you want to practice more than that in a day, two or three brief sessions will do far more good than one long one.

Handlers who are accustomed to using tough training methods will find the techniques in this chapter helpful for therapy dog visits, allowing them to elicit obedience without rough handling.

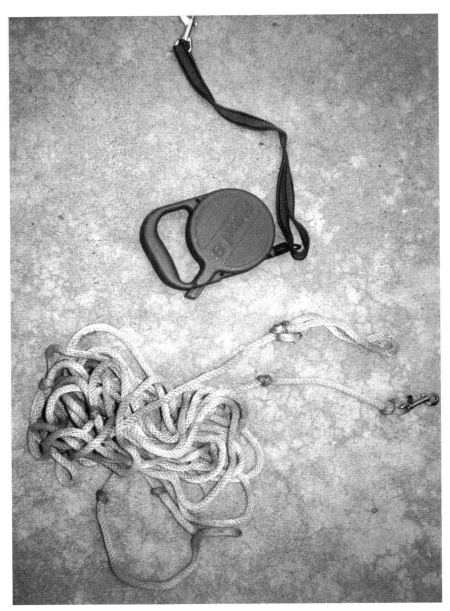

Two effective long lines are shown here.

6.3. COME

The first command to teach your dog is to Come when called. This will help to manage many difficult situations for you. It's an important behavior that starts long before you begin formal training. The way you handle your dog from the beginning will later make this command easy or difficult.

To start, decide on a command word for Come, and use it only when you can make sure the dog will come to you. In other situations when you wish to call your dog, don't use the command word. Instead, you could say "Puppy, puppy, puppy," or just the dog's name with no other words, or even whistle. You could say "Cookie!" or some other word for reward that your dog knows, but don't use such a word and then not give that reward, or eventually the word won't work anymore. Just don't say "Come" unless you're prepared to make sure the dog does come to you. This goes for all command words, if you want your dog to take commands seriously.

The dog needs to be trained to the point of reliably carrying out an action on a single command. When training and working your dog on therapy dog visits, continuous verbal encouragement from you is a plus. The dog must learn to obey without other talk, however, before it's considered trained.

Remember, nothing negative should happen to the dog when it obeys a command, and this goes double for the command to Come. Never call your dog to you and then punish it. Don't call your dog to you and then groom it, unless the dog loves grooming. You may definitely call your dog to dinner, that is, unless you're going to force it to take nasty-tasting medicine before dinner. The event that occurs immediately following a command is what the dog will connect with that command.

Most people do call their dogs and then punish them. Most people who chase a dog that has gotten loose will punish it when they catch it. That's why most dogs don't come when called—their owners have taught them not to!

When you get ready to teach the dog a command for coming when called, the dog should be on leash. Any line attached to a secure collar will do. Say the dog's name to let it know you're talking to it, then with a slight pause after the name, say the command word: "Saint, Come."

Your tone of voice will depend upon the dog. Use a soft tone for a soft dog, but a deeper pitch and firmer tone for a more brassy

To teach the dog the "Come" command, start by putting it on a "Sit" on the end of a long leash. When it is responding dependably, try it off leash. In teaching your therapy dog to come on command, always make sure that it is happy to obey this particular command.

dog that might consider not coming just to see what you would do! Try a higher pitch for a small dog. You'll learn as you work with your dog what it responds to best. Experiment and always listen to yourself. Notice the dog's reactions as you try different voice tones, although before you're ready to start doing therapy dog visits, you'll have to teach this dog to respond to commands given in a pleasant voice and without physical corrections. If possible, train with such tones and handling from the start.

If the dog doesn't come when you call—and doesn't respond to body language such as kneeling down, spreading your arms or running the other way—tug, then loosen, the line and see if that will get the dog started. Encourage and praise as the dog comes to you. If the tug-and-release doesn't get the dog started, keep a good humor and reel the dog in. When you say that command, the dog is going to come to you, whether on its own or because you put its body through the motions.

Losing your temper would be counterproductive. The less tugging the better, because it will distract the dog. If it's too painful or scary (factors that depend on the individual dog), the dog will be too upset to learn. However you get the dog to you, praise and pet the dog and make it feel that with you is a wonderful place to be.

Try your dog off leash when the dog is completely consistent on leash. If the off-leash dog tries to evade you, you must go back to working on leash for a good, long time—probably several weeks. Don't practice off-leash recalls outside a safe enclosure until the dog is 100 percent reliable in the face of any distraction (for some dogs, that will be never). A long line (twenty to forty feet) will let you practice distance around distractions without risking a loose dog.

The recall must be taught over a long period of time, and you must be consistent. If you call your dog and it doesn't come, you must get up from your easy chair and go get the dog. It must Come. If you don't intend to follow through, don't give a command.

One day I was out walking in my neighborhood with one of my dogs on leash and saw two elderly men calling a loose dog. The dog was a clever border collie I knew. He wasn't near traffic, nor was he fleeing in panic—he was moving in a big, border-collie circle! I think he had been trained in a former home. The rather frail men were chasing the dog as best they could, yelling threats at him. Since I felt they wanted to abuse the dog when they caught him, and the dog appeared to be in no danger, I walked on. I'll bet the dog was able to evade them until they were too tired to carry out their threats. I'm sure that was his plan.

Another day I was in my house and the dogs began barking. I looked out the window and saw a chow romping in my front yard, followed by two frightened girls. One was carrying a leash. The dog was heading toward a busy four-lane street, responding to the girls only by moving away from them. I opened the window and told the girls to try running away from the dog, kneeling down and calling it. They did, and the dog stopped going toward the dangerous street. That gave me time to get outside. The dog came up to me curiously, and without touching it I talked to it in a happy voice and walked it back to the kneeling girls, who then put the leash on.

The last example is that of my own well-trained dogs in a silly moment. I used to take all three dogs along in the car on cool mornings for Saint to work a scent track. The other two dogs knew they would be staying in the car. One morning Angel decided to lead a play expedition with her faithful sidekick, Star. When I opened the car door, both dogs jumped out and took off across the empty parking lot to a hill that looked like fun. My first instinct was to scream at them and chase them. That's the natural reaction of any panicked owner. But then training—mine—kicked in, and I stopped. I called to them in my happiest voice. They whirled around and came to me. I praised them for coming. I encouraged them back into the car, and I did not punish them. Of course I did give them some review about not jumping out of the car later, but not then. It was a one-time problem that hasn't happened since.

As these examples show, if your dog isn't trained, you may be able to get the dog to come to you in an emergency—but you will first have to get control of yourself and use the right handling in spite of your emotions! If your dog is trained, you can still fail by not using what you know—and your dog's life can be the price of failure. In coming when called, as in all dog training, controlling ourselves is absolutely necessary if we wish to control our dogs.

With any off-leash training you do, be certain that your dog is under control or that you work in an escape-proof enclosure. Give your dog more freedom as it becomes more reliable.

6.4. SIT-STAY

Probably the next thing most educated dogs learn is the Sit-Stay. In this position you have the dog's attention to teach it other things.

This command should be taught gently. Treats can help in early training for the Sit, especially with a puppy. I don't use food in training most commands, but it's okay to do so as long as you gradually phase the food out. Otherwise the dog will only obey when you have food—and that's not a trained dog!

If you've properly conditioned your dog to being handled, you can use physical manipulation to teach the dog what you mean by Sit. You can even sit down beside the dog for early lessons. You may not need a leash in the beginning.

The exact physical maneuvers depend upon the dog's size and shape. Be gentle. First the dog needs to learn what Sit means. Gradually you'll use a firmer tone, and work with the dog on leash.

My favorite way to put the dog into a Sit, and the gentlest I know (other than dangling food just over a puppy's head), is done with two hands. One palm holds the dog's chin and pushes up, while the other pushes gently down on the rear. If the dog is huge or confused, the rear hand can go behind the knees to gently bend them so the rear goes down. You can hook your thumb through the collar to help you steady the chin. Later your palm moving upward becomes a Sit signal.

The dog should learn the Sit before you start using the leash to force it into a Sit. It's not fair to jerk on the collar if the dog doesn't understand what you want it to do. Until the dog does know—and any time afterward when you want to use gentle handling—put it into position with your hands. If later you feel that a jerk on the collar is appropriate, remember that good timing, not pain or fear, is what makes physical discipline work.

As your dog learns, add the Stay command after the Sit and gradually lengthen the time you require the dog to Sit. As you say "Stay," give a hand signal. I hold my palm flat, facing the dog, and move my hand from side to side just in front of the dog's nose. As you move away to teach the dog to Stay without you there, you can reinforce your verbal Stay with a hand held out, palm toward the dog.

Use a watch, or count the time silently ("One thousand, two thousand," etc.). It might take three months or so of daily practice

The conditioning to handling Sit, with the handler restraining the dog, is the first step to a gentle "Sit" command.

to work up to one minute at thirty feet—longer for a puppy. Eventually a five-minute Sit-Stay, with you going out of sight, would be a good goal for an advanced therapy dog. This might take a year of practicing every day, and a mature dog.

A Sit longer than five minutes is not necessary, since for longer than that you should leave your dog in a Down. The Sit is somewhat uncomfortable for a dog to hold. On a slippery floor, such as those often found in facilities, a seated dog has to continually work to keep its front feet from sliding forward.

During any Stay exercise, keep your attention on the dog throughout. Giving your full attention is a skill you will need for handling a therapy dog. Handler attention is one of the secrets of success in dog training, and takes practice and effort to develop in yourself.

If your dog is well conditioned to your voice, verbal encouragement will help it learn to Stay. Praise the dog as it works well and warn the dog when it starts to break without permission ("No, Stay."). Learn to recognize the signs that your dog is about to do something, and learn to react in time. These skills are vital in therapy dog work.

In practice Stays, I don't let the dog get up until after I return, stand beside it for fifteen seconds and give a release word. I say "Saint, Okay!" and at the same time give the dog a signal. (I cast my arms outward as the Okay signal.) This way, if I happen to use the word "okay" in conversation without the signal, the dog won't take it as a release. Remember to release when it's time, not when you see the dog about to break! If the dog is about to break, that's the time to help it Stay. The extra fifteen seconds of holding the Stay after you return will help your dog avoid the fault of breaking the command too soon. I continue to practice this extra time occasionally, even with a fully-trained dog.

If your dog breaks the Stay, simply put the dog back and restart the time. Don't punish the dog, or you might accidentally condition it to run from you when it breaks a Stay. On therapy dog visits the dog must sometimes move from a Stay. You don't want your dog to run, or to stay there and cause someone to fall when you didn't see the person coming in time, but the dog did. Dogs are much more alert to movement than people are. If you handle your dog carefully in training and practicing Stays, the dog will learn to—when in trouble—either move slightly and look to you for further instructions, or come calmly to you.

Bill places Star into a "Sit" with his palm under her chin and his left hand pressing down her rear.

Here Bill's right thumb is hooked through Star's collar and his left hand exerts pressure behind the knees to put her into the "Sit." This maneuver gives the handler more control, but is still gentle.

The hand signal for the "Sit-Stay" command demonstrated.

"Okay!" release.

122

When training in public, if you see someone approaching to pet the dog, release the dog from command before it can break, unless you can nicely ask the person to wait until the dog finishes the exercise. You need people to pet your therapy dog. You can practice commands any time, but friendly strangers to pet the dog aren't always available. If you think asking them to wait would turn them away, release the dog right then for petting. Petting comes first with a therapy dog.

If the dog breaks the command before you can release it, have the dog do the Stay again, after petting. Restart the clock so it gets no credit for the time it did Stay—that's the penalty. Don't punish or correct the dog for breaking a Stay to be friendly. Another way to handle this is to move to the dog's side and hold it in its Stay position while it's being petted. Thank the person for helping you train your therapy dog! As your "Stay" work progresses, you will gradually move farther away, and remove the leash, but don't rush either of these steps.

Some dogs don't work well off leash. You should probably teach such a dog the off-leash work anyway, always in a location where the dog can't get loose and into trouble. On therapy dog visits, however, a dog that doesn't work well off leash should stay on leash. The off-leash training will simply give you additional control. If the dog's instincts or training aren't good for off-leash work, it's no problem for a therapy dog to remain on leash at all times on visits. Do what's best for you and your dog, even if other handlers take their dogs off leash. Some people work their dogs off leash when they shouldn't because they can't control the dogs on leash. This is not an acceptable reason! Every therapy dog handler must be proficient at the skill of handling a dog on leash. There's no substitute for practice in learning this skill.

6.5. DOWN-STAY

You may want to teach the Down-Stay exercise to the dog next, because it's such a good control position. Like the Sit-Stay, the foundation for the Down-Stay is the time you spend cuddling, handling, holding and petting your dog. If your dog has trouble with Stays, the cuddling time will be just as important as training time to achieve your eventual success. Stays are extremely helpful for therapy dogs.

The hands-on "Down" position conditions the dog before it is taught "Down" as a command.

How you teach the Down may depend upon other work you plan to do with your dog. For example, herding dogs have a specific command and even a whistle tone for the Down. They're taught this command with force, to obey instantly at a distance from the handler when in the exciting act of chasing livestock. Similarly, competition obedience dogs lose points for slow drops. However, your therapy dog does not have to drop quickly. A herding dog drops on natural turf, and a competition dog drops on grass or a rubber mat, but therapy dogs often have to drop on pavement or linolem floors. Therefore, if your dog doesn't need a fast drop for another job, it's okay to teach the Down from a Sit, which is easier and gentler than teaching it from running or standing. Later you can practice Downs in motion on soft surfaces, if you wish.

The Down position is submissive. You don't want to intimidate your dog and make it hate this command. If you teach the Down from the Sit, one end is already down, so you can gently push down and back on the shoulders, or pull the front legs forward. If the dog flops on its side or back, let that count as a Down. In time the dog will gain confidence and stay more upright. As long as both ends remain down, the dog is allowed to shift its weight. It must hold its position and remain facing the same direction, but it may change weight from one hip to the other, etc. There is no good reason to demand military precision when all you need is a steady, reliable Down-Stay.

Watch your tone on the Down command. Handlers tend to use a mean tone on this command that's offensive in public and expresses the wrong attitude. You don't want to browbeat the dog into submission. You need a dog that obeys happily. When your dog is steady enough, practice petting it when it is in the "Down-Stay."

You can start the Down-Stay work soon after the Sit, and develop the time on them together. You can practice first the Sit and then the Down each day if you wish. Practice at a time set aside for practice, or at a convenient time, such as while preparing the dog's food—as long as your attention is on your dog to reposition it immediately if it breaks, to restart the time if necessary and to release the dog when the time is up. Work up to three minutes on the Down, ten minutes for an advanced, mature dog.

As you teach the word "Down" (or your chosen command word), teach a signal, too. When I'm next to the dog, my Down signal is two fingers, usually on the right hand, starting in front of the dog's nose and guiding it to the ground.

Bill's left hand pushes down and back on Star's shoulders to put her into a "Down" from the "Sit" position.

The "Down" signal.

On both Sit- and Down-Stays, the out-of-sight work is accomplished gradually, and only when the dog is mature. Training to that degree is valuable but not essential to therapy dog work. Corners are useful when training out-of-sight Stays. You can be close but out of sight around a corner. In the earliest stage I enjoy setting up a mirror so the dogs and I can see each other in it. It teaches them to use a mirror, and also that when the mirror isn't there, I might be just around that corner!

6.6. HEEL

The Heel command begins to prepare your dog for the outside world. If your dog isn't used to a leash, the first step is to introduce it as a pleasant, not scary, experience. Pushing the dog to accept the leash too quickly can create long-term problems. Letting it drag the leash helps, starting with short sessions and never letting the dog reach the point of panic.

The first time you put the leash on and hold the other end, work in a safe, quiet place. Encourage the dog to go the way you want to go, but use only restraint, with no force.

The perfect, total-attention heeling of the obedience ring is not necessary for therapy dog work. It's okay to teach it to your therapy dog if you wish, but use a different command for walking the dog without total attention, such as when your dog is relating to other people.

Heel refers to where the dog is supposed to be: at your left side. If you're moving, it means to keep pace with you in that position. If you're stopped, Heel means to get to your left and to Sit. If you don't want the dog to Sit, you can give a different position command (such as Stand) as the dog reaches the Heel location. Teach the dog where Heel is in a positive manner. You want the dog to feel secure when it is next to you.

You must keep your attention on the dog from the time you say "Heel" until you release the dog from command, even if in informal work you choose to let the dog look around and sniff a bit. It must pay enough attention to maintain position at your side. The fact that the dog has to pay some attention makes this a useful command for when there are distractions you must pass. The Heel command gives the dog something to do besides get into mischief.

Ultimately you'll teach the dog to Heel with the leash loose. This becomes the transition to teaching the dog to Heel off leash.

It's useful to practice heeling occasionally. Intricate footwork, weaving around posts and turning in different directions while keeping the dog's attention will build your control over your dog. Since therapy dogs work in front of the handler and interact with other people while still obeying the handler, I also practice weaving around posts with the dog walking ahead of me on light lead tension and verbal cues.

Besides using Heel to take your dog's mind off a distraction, Heel is an excellent warm-up to calm an energetic dog before entering a facility. It shifts the dog into working gear. That is probably why it's the first exercise in each category of obedience competition. At its most sophisticated, heeling is like dancing with your dog. If you have trouble giving your dog steady foot movements to work with, you might try practicing with music.

As long as you're gentle with your dog, you can get as fancy with heeling as you like. If you find that your dog forges ahead of you, go more slowly, stop often, make frequent about-turns and left turns, and back up a step or two now and then. If the dog tends to lag, walk more quickly in practice. Lagging can be caused by training too harshly and trying to make the dog learn precision too fast. Heeling is much more difficult for the dog than it appears. Give lots of encouragement, and if you don't wish to train for precision— which would likely require some skillful coaching from an obedience expert—don't expect the dog to work with precision. Steady heeling is needed for therapy dog work, but precision is not.

When your dog has learned to Heel on leash, gradually teach it to Heel off leash as well. This gives better control and reduces the need for tough corrections when working the dog in public. The rule for off-leash work is that if your dog shows any lapse in reliability, put the leash back on immediately.

A lot of factors go into the transition to off-leash work, and some are breed specific. For example, dogs bred for herding, pointing and retrieving tend to have a desire to please the owner and therefore make a good transition to off-leash work. They were bred for jobs that cannot be done on leash. On the other hand, some dogs may need to be so thoroughly patterned to each command that it doesn't occur to them to disobey, and you may need a long line or other means of correcting or stopping the dog.

Every well-trained dog should respond to the "Heel" command. For the therapy dog, response to "Heel" need not take the precise format normally associated with the obedience ring. Good heeling is not as easy to achieve as it appears and the therapy dog and handler should practice regularly on this important part of their joint skill.

6.7. TRAINING COLLARS

While teaching your dog to Heel on leash, you're making decisions about how to use the leash with your dog, how to give corrections, what type of training collar to use, and how to train your dog so that it will eventually obey your commands without a leash. No one training collar is right for all dogs. Some trainers who are physically adept can work all dogs on the same type of collar, but that ability depends upon skill and knowledge that most people lack.

The gentlest restraint on a dog is a harness. A harness doesn't give you good control over the dog, unless you're much stronger than the dog. However, the harness takes pressure off the dog's throat, and I use it with my small Spitz, now that she's trained and mature. Many small dogs cannot endure much pressure on the larynx from a collar, and a harness can also be good when introducing a puppy to the leash.

The next gentlest restraint is a buckle, or other nonslip collar. Your dog should wear such a collar with identification tags. Take it off only when the dog is in a crate or in some other situation where the collar could be a hazard. Some dogs can be trained on a buckle collar. It will at least give you control around the house.

The next, more forceful collar is one of the various limited-slip collars. Some are designed to work from either side, an advantage with a beginning dog that doesn't yet know to work on your left. These collars must be fitted carefully, both for the fully-tight fit and for the loose fit. They can be great for sensitive dogs.

The slip collar—also called choke collar—of chain, fabric or leather is the most traditional training collar. It must fit well and be put on the dog the right way. Have the pet shop or your obedience instructor show you how to use it. Get the smallest size that will go on over the dog's head, because extra collar length delays communication with your dog. The dog can back out of a slip collar, and it only works from one direction, so it requires skill from the handler. There's some risk of injury to people petting the dog if the dog is wearing a slip collar and the handler isn't alert. If your dog needs this collar on visits, stay alert for people catching a hand in the collar when it's loose, since tightening it could then hurt them.

The pinch or prong collar is made of metal and is a severe training collar. It should not be used without the supervision of an instructor. A prong collar should never be left on an unattended dog for even one minute. Neither the slip collar nor the prong collar

Some types of collars used in training therapy dogs.

Bill positions Star in the "Stand."

131

should be worn by a dog riding in a car. In an accident the collar could catch on something and the dog could die in agony.

The prong collar exerts several times more force than a slip collar, more force than most dogs need. It should be used only with a dog that has little body sensitivity and never on an aggressive dog. The slip collar is the correct collar for an aggressive dog; the pinch collar can intensify such a dog's desire to bite.

The prong collar isn't harmful when used correctly. However, it must not be used on therapy dog visits, and a dog that needs a prong collar for training may need to be several years old and highly trained before being considered for therapy dog work.

Another collar unacceptable on visits is the spike collar. While the prong collar has smooth prongs that cannot penetrate the skin resting against the dog's neck, the spikes of a spike collar are sharp-pointed. Another type of spike collar, used on livestock-guarding dogs, has spikes that point outward, to protect the dog from predators. The sharp points of either type of spike collar would endanger people on therapy dog visits.

The head halter is popular with some trainers. If you wish to try this with your dog, work with an instructor. The dog will have to learn reliable control on a slip collar, buckle collar or harness before starting therapy dog visits, since a head halter would be disturbing to the public eye.

Humans have a tendency to escalate the amount of force when training dogs. Don't be this kind of trainer. Use the least force necessary, lots of encouragement and the gentlest equipment possible to get your dog to respond. The equipment is only a tool for control, and does not motivate the dog. Your goal is to teach the dog to respond to you.

6.8. STAND FOR PETTING

The next exercise needed for basic work is the Stand. This is a Stay, but with the addition that the dog must accept petting. Therapy dogs must also accept petting in the Sit and Down positions, but the Stand is the hardest.

The Stand is not a long Stay. One minute is long enough, although you could work up gradually to about four minutes if you wish. This exercise is so hard for some dogs that if you add time too quickly they'll give up. If that happens, on this or any exercise,

"Sit" for petting.

"Down" for petting.

take a break for a few days or weeks. When you come back to training the exercise, be more positive and gentle and less demanding. Food treats help rehabilitate work on an exercise you've messed up by pushing the dog too hard.

The Stand needs to be taught on signal and verbal command, without wrestling the dog into position, because holding the dog distracts it. My signal for Stand is to hold my right hand in front of the dog's nose, palm flat and toward the dog, with fingers spread. On Stand as well as on Stay, teaching a signal when the dog first learns the verbal command makes it much easier. Word and signal should be given at the same time.

You can help your dog into a Stand by hooking your right thumb through the collar and your right hand under the chin as for the Sit, and holding your left hand, palm flat and facing down, against the front of the dog's right hind leg where it meets the body. This prevents the dog from sitting or lying down. Get your hands away as quickly as you can.

When walking the dog into a Stand, I move forward one step with my left foot as I give the signal. The dog then has distance to stop, put its feet into a comfortable stance and Stand.

If you find that your dog creeps forward on this command, one gentle correction is to give the signal with your right hand while blocking forward movement of the dog's right hind leg with your left hand. I like to minimize use of the leash in teaching this exercise, as it is even more distracting to a well-conditioned dog than hands are.

The Stand in obedience competition allows you to pose your dog if you wish, which is quite useful with a therapy dog. Generally the best Stand position for the non-show dog (conformation dogs need to stand in the most flattering pose for each breed) is with each leg vertical, not stretched out. Take the feet one at a time and move them into this position. Dogs react best if you first lightly touch the back and run your hand gently down the body and leg to the foot.

The petting portion of this exercise is introduced after the dog is steady. Before trying it, have someone pet your dog while it does Sit- and Down-Stays. If the dog has any trouble accepting petting in these two positions, it's not ready for petting on the Stand. If the dog shows aggression when the person approaches, forget about therapy dog work for now, and get expert help. The same applies if the dog runs in panic from the person.

Both aggression and shyness come in degrees. Aggressiveness should always be evaluated, since when it gets worse it can be so dangerous. A slight degree of shyness that is not accompanied by any sign of aggression is less serious. A dog that can hold position and accept petting with no sign of aggression, even if it seems to want to leave, is not genuinely shy. Just be sure to give it lots of low-stress social experience.

If the dog tends to break the Stay to go wagging toward the stranger, don't give a harsh correction—that would be correcting the dog when it is in the act of being friendly. This dog's heart is in the right place. Just practice faithfully and help the dog hold steady. It may need to be older before its Stand will be reliable—some dogs mature late. Don't rush the dog or use violent corrections, because there is no substitute for adequate practice and maturity. You could ruin the dog. Handled correctly, the friendly, bouncy youngster may well have a longer working life than a less energetic dog, so you'll be ahead in the long run. Keep practicing, and appreciate your dog's good qualities.

6.9. GREETING

The therapy dog needs one more basic control exercise. It's the Greeting.

For this exercise, I tell my dog, "Go say 'Hi'!" You can use any phrase you like, but it makes sense to include "go," which is used in commands that send the dog away from you. I'm not sure, though, that I would consider this a command. The therapy dog should have some say in whether or not it wants to interact with a particular person. I don't believe a dog should be forced to give love. In training you may occasionally insist, when you absolutely know the person won't hurt or scare your dog, but in public give the dog a vote. Dogs know things about other people that people don't know.

What the dog should do on this cue is to move toward the person you indicate with a hand gesture. For a timid dog, this lets the dog go up to the person instead of the person coming to the dog. The dog will find this much less stressful.

If your dog is reluctant to approach others, you can carry treats and hand the person a treat to give to the dog (tell the person how to do it safely). Ask the person to kneel down; this will help make the dog feel less nervous. If possible, take a timid dog on outings

The Greeting.

with an outgoing, friendly dog the timid dog likes. This can have a profound influence in encouraging a backward dog to join the petting.

With an overly friendly dog, the greeting teaches the dog not to go up to people until you say to. Don't jerk the dog back, just hold or pull it back. Your "Go say 'Hi'! becomes the release giving the friendly dog permission to do what it wishes to do, which is to go greet that person. This cue is necessary because not everyone wants to be touched or approached by a dog. Some people are afraid of dogs, dislike them, are allergic or are wearing clothes they don't want decorated with dog hair.

These exercises will give you the control you need to work with your dog in public, if your dog has a friendly temperament. You would be wise to test your control over your dog in situations in which you and the dog can be judged objectively, such as obedience classes, matches or other tests. This is especially true with the first dog you train.

I'm an advocate of training for all dogs, certainly any dog that lives with me. However, many untrained dogs are functioning well on visits to facilities. Some dogs are easy to handle. All sorts of different arrangements work for someone, somewhere. If you're involved in such an arrangement, I want this book to help you, not offend you. However, given full knowledge and the choice between having a trained dog for therapy dog visits or an untrained one, I think most handlers and facilities would choose a trained dog. When training is tailored to the dog, it never does any harm.

If you are already doing therapy dog visits with little or no training, consider getting some. It makes life safer and better for the dog. Instead of being restricted and perhaps carried or pulled around, the trained dog can be told what you want it to do and praised for doing it. Such a therapy dog experiences less stress, and with the right handler will get better and better at its work over time. This also results in advantages for everyone else. The handler is reasonably free from worry about the dog hurting anyone and feels a partnership with the dog. The staff is not inconvenienced by the dog's presence in the facility. People are comfortable around the dog and can bond to it quickly. The visitation program can be stable, because the dog enjoys visits with reduced risk of burnout, and the staff has no reason to want to cancel the program. Since it's the long-term, regular program of therapy dog visits that serves everyone best, training is the key factor in this worthwhile endeavor.

The development of good social skills is imperative in a therapy dog. Many of these require to be learned in public places.

7

Social Skills

THIS CHAPTER is entitled "Social Skills," rather than "Socialization," because therapy dogs do their jobs by interacting with people. Just standing in the facility calmly can be achieved through socialization, but interacting and communicating with people require social skills.

Dogs that guide the blind are trained in public, because it is felt that they must work in real situations in order to learn. If the situation is set up to simulate reality but isn't real, the dog knows the difference. I believe this is also true of therapy dogs.

In a class, the dog can learn commands, be tested on control and work on special problems that particular dog has—such as a bad response to other dogs. Basic control skills are necessary before going out in public with the dog, but some skills beyond this can only be learned by working the dog in real situations. As much as it is safe to do so, we need to train our therapy dogs in these real situations.

A dog knows the difference between a normal person and a person with an emotional or mental impairment. While an unsocialized dog might react negatively to such a person—a problem you would then need to work out with training—many therapy dogs have consistently shown special understanding and tolerance when working with impaired people. This is not automatic, but requires a well-socialized dog.

Dogs also seem to understand the difference between the deliberate act of a coherent person and the behavior of an impaired person—or an accident involving any type of person. Dogs are usually very forgiving in such situations, if they feel the handler will prevent the incident from going too far. If you don't protect your dog, the dog's understanding of the differences between normal people and those with special problems could mean that a bad experience would make that dog especially distrust impaired people. Dogs clearly can detect differences and emotional states in humans, but how a dog acts on its knowledge of differences among people depends on how that dog has been treated by and around each type of person.

Dogs can't be tested in controlled situations to find out how they would act in real therapy dog situations. The dog will always know the difference. Instead of elaborate testing, handlers must learn to give their dogs proper support, and be alert for early signs of trouble. Almost every problem will show signs before anything serious happens, if you know what to watch for.

Your goal when working your therapy dog in public is to teach the dog to work under control and interact with people. Good skills with "normal" people—the full range of human beings encountered in everyday life—form the foundation for helping people in facilities. A therapy dog and handler need to interact regularly with people of all types.

7.1. BE IN CONTROL: NEVER ENDANGER THE PUBLIC

Before taking a dog out in public to work on social skills, you must have enough control over the dog to ensure that other people won't be in danger at any time. That's why basic control work comes before training for social skills.

If you don't feel totally in control of your dog, don't start working on social skills around other people yet. I don't want to encourage anyone with a dog that isn't safe for other people and their dogs to be around, to take that dog out in public in the name of therapy dog work. You would accomplish nothing by doing so, and you could get your dog and yourself into trouble.

One way to test yourself is to work your dog on its commands and "keep score." Out of ten times that you leave your dog on a Sit-Stay and call the dog (only one command allowed!), how many times does the dog come? It should be eight or nine out of ten before you can consider the dog reliable. Whenever the dog fails to come, it should sit right there and wait to be called again, with no lack of control. It should come on the second command.

If your dog is that steady on the command in varied settings, it has learned the exercise. Go through a similar scoring process on all the basic control exercises. Work under conditions similar to the distractions you expect in the places you want to take your dog.

Such testing should not take place in one massive session. You might do two or three repetitions in a practice session, but doing ten at a time could make your dog depressed. Instead, look at your dog's responses over one or two weeks of practice sessions. Does the dog consistently obey each command? When the dog fails to obey a command, does it ever go out of control?

Before working the dog in public, you must also consider temperament. If you've trained your dog in the basics, you've had the chance to observe the dog in many situations. How does it act at the veterinarian's office? Does it react negatively under any circumstances against children or men? Does it growl or lunge at other dogs. If the dog dislikes any type of person or other dog, get the help of a qualified trainer to make sure the dog is thoroughly under control and to help you evaluate the dog's temperament.

Some dogs simply aren't suited for therapy dog work. Others need lots of training first, perhaps more than you want to give. If you have doubts, even ''funny feelings'' you can't put into words, get help. A person's relationship with a dog is largely nonverbal. You may know something about your dog through this language without words.

Always keep in mind the limits of your dog's control (no matter how advanced, every dog has limits), and don't relax your attention when in public.

7.2. BE IN CONTROL: NEVER ENDANGER THE DOG

Just as important as ensuring the safety of others is protecting your dog at all times. Many dog owners fail in this and ruin a good therapy dog. When the owner doesn't control a dog's experiences, the dog can develop bad attitudes and behaviors. Everything that happens to a dog influences how that dog will turn out. The dog

The well-trained therapy dog is steady around other dogs and different animals. Meeting dogs owned by others in a public setting is a very beneficial drill for the new or experienced therapy dog.

can't tell you what has happened—you must know. This essential part of handling a therapy dog makes it a twenty-four-hour-a-day responsibility.

Control over the dog's enviroment begins at home, making sure no one ever abuses the dog and that the dog has no opportunities to kill or injure other animals. Not only could these experiences prevent your dog from becoming a therapy dog, they could lead the dog to do something that would cause authorities to intervene and destroy the dog—or a neighbor to shoot or poison the dog out of fear.

Don't allow your dog around people who are drinking alcohol (and don't work your dog when you're drinking) or using recreational drugs—it makes people's behavior too erratic. Don't leave the dog alone with young children. Parents may think this restriction unreasonable, but it's necessary. A child isn't capable of empathy until between five and seven years of age and might do anything to a dog—especially when no adult is watching. An abused dog might then bite and forever after dislike children. This is unfair to both the child and the dog.

The dog shouldn't be put at the mercy of anyone you can't totally trust to treat the dog well. You don't want a therapy dog to feel it must defend itself from people; you want it to look to you to protect it, and you want it to trust you. To achieve this, you must be consistent and faithful about protecting your dog.

7.3. ALL TYPES OF PEOPLE AND SITUATIONS

Your goal is to work your dog around all the people and situations you might expect to encounter in therapy dog work or in your normal lifestyle with your dog. At the same time, you don't want to put the dog into any situation that might create or reinforce fears.

Give your dog experiences with people of all races, people wearing unusual costumes, men with varying degrees of facial hair, children and anyone else you know to be harmless. Give everyone the same respect. If you do, your dog will learn to do so as well. Let the dog know that differences in people are okay.

I teach my dogs on our outings that the dog will not be held responsible for commands given by other people. If someone passing by or petting the dog tells it to do something, I simply don't follow through on that command. If necessary, I give the dog a conflicting command. The dog must know to obey the handler, not just anyone in the area. Some people think a dog is a machine for them to give orders to, just to see it obey. I feel it's a service to help such people learn that this is not the case. If you want your dog to obey commands given by others, you'll need to practice that with the other person holding the leash. Dominant dogs, dogs with no protection instinct and dogs that must at times be handled by others may all benefit from this training.

I teach my dogs that social interaction is with other people, but commands come from me. When necessary, each of them cooperates well with someone who needs to take the leash, such as at the veterinarian's office. Make a careful choice about how to handle your dog, and then be consistent.

Whenever you see a situation that's unusual, but safe, use it to educate your dog. For example, one morning I was walking with Star and came to a wooden stage in front of a neighborhood business for an outdoor performance later in the day. With the manager's permission, Star and I walked on it and I called her across it, until she learned that it was safe. Dog trainers continually watch for such opportunities.

In accustoming your dog to new situations, use your commands. Help your dog by telling it what to do. When the dog does what you say, it has success. Every time this happens, the dog develops more faith in you and in obeying you as a way to cope with life. This encourages the dog to look to you when it doesn't know what to do. If you plan to be there for your therapy dog when it's working in a facility, this is exactly the attitude you want the dog to have.

When working your dog on commands in public and in new situations, avoid being stubborn. This is the time to further develop the give-and-take between you and your dog and to develop the dog's initiative. You want this dog to become your partner and to tell you things you can't perceive with human senses. Since communication often requires persistence before the other party understands, give your dog much encouragement in this area.

Working in public will involve situations when the dog sees a hazard before you do, and the dog must disobey a command. If the dog makes an especially clever judgment call, be sure to praise the dog. Once I was walking with Star and stepped out from behind a parked van onto a lightly traveled road. Star pulled me back—she'd seen a car coming that I didn't see. She got lots of praise!

Another time, I had my dogs on a Stay at a spot where the sidewalk jutted into a parking lot, when a big truck drove to the

The poise of a therapy dog is enhanced by taking advantage of training opportunities in public places and doing familiar things under unfamiliar circumstances. Here Bill and Star make excellent use of a short concrete staircase with an open railing to practice heeling and "Sit-Stays".

edge on its way around. The dogs moved. They were right—the truck could have easily rolled over that curb and hit them. I had them repeat the Stay, but not so near the edge. That's give-and-take, with the handler keeping control.

When your dog messes up a command, you should generally make it repeat the exercise in exactly the same situation—in other words, put it exactly where it was in the first place for a Stay if it moved. However, if that place was unsafe, moving the dog before repeating the Stay is an ideal way to encourage your dog to show you when something's wrong, without making it an excuse for disobedience.

Be considerate of your dog. If I want to take one of my house dogs out to practice Stays on a cold day, I put a coat on the dog before asking it to Down for five minutes on icy pavement. On a hot day, I work only on pavement that's been in the shade for hours. If your commands are reasonable, the dog will try harder to please you. At the same time, everyone who sees you training will feel good about your treatment of the dog. This makes your work far more acceptable in public.

Look at things from the dog's perspective. Once I asked Saint to jump into an obstacle on a playground. He kept refusing; I kept insisting. He finally did it, and I saw what he'd realized all along: it was too narrow inside for him to land. I guess I expected him to do a handstand! I apologized to him. Dogs understand when you admit you were wrong. When you treat them more considerately the next time, they learn to trust you.

The handling skills you develop working your dog in public will carry over to therapy dog visits. You need to know what your dog is thinking. It's not easy, but spending the time and learning the give-and-take with your dog will make it happen. Don't hesitate to drop down and get your eyes to the level of the dog's eyes to see what it sees. Watch your dog carefully, and constantly. Since dogs use body language instead of words, time spent watching the dog is the equivalent of time spent listening to a human. Watch your dog interact with other dogs and other people. When you are watching and not involved with the interaction, you can learn things you would never learn any other way.

In training classes and competitive events, the "world" is structured and controlled. In the real world, you and your dog will develop skills for therapy dog visits that you can't learn in structured settings. You need the structure first. Then get out and learn to apply the skills in real life.

Wheels—the successful therapy dog must be comfortable around them at all times. The dog will encounter them everywhere in nursing homes and other facilities where its services are required. Wheelchairs, carts, screens and other pieces of equipment will roll by from every direction and the therapy dog must be prepared. If you can work with a shopping cart, heeling the dog alongside or taking it for a spin now and then, you'll find your dog unfazed on a therapy visit as life "rolls" by.

7.4. LEARN TO "READ" PEOPLE

One of the basic skills you'll work on when out with your dog is the ability to "read" people. You and your dog both need this skill. It's a complex task that depends as much on people's body language as on what they say.

Watch people closely and listen to them carefully when out with your dog. At first, don't let your dog go near anyone unless the person asks. As you gain skill, you can sometimes give the dog the greeting cue when the person has indicated he or she wants to be near the dog but hasn't actually asked. You'll learn to respond to things like the person reaching a hand toward the dog, or looking at the dog in a longing way. When you aren't sure, ask the person if he or she likes dogs. If you make a wrong decision and take the dog near people who don't want you to, you'll learn to read this in their faces and body language. Then, of course, calmly move your dog away.

You don't need to jump into working on social skills all at once. You can start taking your dog out on walks to practice basic control work, teaching the dog to work around people. To some extent you'll always do this; practicing basic commands in public is important throughout the dog's career. As you work with the dog, people will naturally be interested, and social interaction will develop. Remember never to correct the dog when it's in the act of being friendly.

7.5. COURTESY IN PUBLIC

In public you'll observe people showing various emotions when they see your dog. Just as a dog learns to guide a blind person by bumping the trainer into things, you'll learn by observing and responding to these emotions. You must have enormous respect for other people's feelings about your dog. Therefore, courtesy in public includes not only such things as picking up feces if your dog has an accident (which should rarely happen, if you take the dog to relieve itself in an acceptable place before and after each outing), but extreme consideration for other people in every way. If this seems unreasonable, remember that you're practicing to work with people who can't always tell you how they feel, and who may have no choice about being around your dog when you enter their facility.

148

Use the time when you and your dog are out in public to learn to "read" people. Sharpen your powers of observation to determine who signals a desire to interact with your dog. This can be a valuable sixth sense in a facility when nonverbal communication is often involved.

The therapy dog must always be a good will ambassador for its work and for the good all dogs represent and a source of pride to those around it.

Learn good skills by working with people who can tell you if you're bothering them. The more you learn to read people's expressions and respond instantly to their feelings, the better a handler you'll become.

When you look into people's faces to smile at them, observe their expressions. If they look nervous about the dog, don't approach any nearer. I routinely stop when walking a large dog in my neighborhood shopping center and have the dog do a Down-Stay until any nervous-looking person has passed. If you were going to the grocery store or to buy a pair of shoes and were afraid of dogs, and there was a big one right in your path, perhaps coming right at you, how would you feel? What if the handler gave you a friendly smile and had the dog lie down well out of your way until you got into the store or to your car? What if you were an elderly person and unsure of your footing? You might like dogs, but you don't know this one. It could easily cause you to fall on this hard pavement, maybe break a hip, have to go to the hospital, never walk again and end up in a nursing home—how would you feel?

What if you were a mom or dad carrying a baby—or a grandparent with your grandchild—and perhaps riding herd over one or two other young children running ahead and exploring? You know that the first thing those young'uns are going to do is run up and touch that dog, and you don't know anything about that dog or its owner. If that handler and dog showed you in a friendly way that they cared about your needs and your feelings and that everything was under control, would you mind the dog being there? Probably not.

Working your dog around the public means reaching out to other people and learning to control the situation. This skill will be exactly the same when you start working in facilities with your dog. You must master it, and practice it regularly, if you are to be effective.

The way your dog looks will make your job more or less difficult. It took me years to learn how to put people at ease around Saint, with his large, black, short-haired, erect-eared body. On the other hand, it's rare to find anyone who is afraid of small, white, fluffy Angel.

Until you can put everyone at ease around your dog, don't try therapy dog visits. You'll find it easier to master other handling skills before you have to master this one, which is one of the hardest, though absolutely essential. If you have a choice of eligible dogs to work with as therapy dogs, start with the dog that looks the least scary—people have every right not to have to feel afraid.

7.6. PUT PEOPLE AT EASE

As you move from practicing with your dog in private to working in public, your control work will be the means of putting people at ease around your dog. Seeing that you can control the dog will make most people willing to have it around. If they're afraid, move the dog away from them and have it do a Down.

Ironically, the dog that obeys commands not only relaxes well-meaning people who fear dogs, but also inspires the respect of bad guys! If the dog obeys you, they don't know what else it might be trained to do for you. You won't get sued when out with a dog on leash that always obeys you and never hurts anyone, yet you'll have all the protection most people need.

After control, the next most important element in putting people at ease around your dog is for you to smile at them. If a sinister-looking person is following you and you don't want to put him or her at ease, don't look at the person. Leave doubt about your attitude and discourage interaction by giving no expression. But if you meet a nonthreatening person when out with your dog, a smile can be like a bridge of goodwill.

Why is it so important for you to smile? First, people instinctively know that your dog will probably back up your attitude. Trained or not, dogs tend to be allowed to do what their owners like, and prevented from doing what their owners don't like.

Second, when I smile at a person while working my dog, I express confidence that I can easily control the dog. A smile combined with obvious control gives people confidence in a handler. Be sure to exercise that control, though. A smiling handler with an out-of-control dog will look like an unreliable idiot!

Why take the time and trouble to be nice to people you meet in public when training a therapy dog? There are many reasons. One of the most basic is that people don't have to let you be there with a dog. If you're in a public place, people in charge can either ask you to leave, or make a new rule: "No dogs allowed." It happens all the time, all over the world, mostly because of inconsiderate dog owners. Therapy dog handlers must be just the opposite. In the process, you'll win friends for dogs as well as access to more places to practice with your therapy dog.

Therapy dogs don't, in most locales, have the right to go absolutely anywhere their handlers want to take them. This privilege is extended to certain trained dogs upon whose help a disabled owner's safety depends. Therapy dog handlers don't have this need. You do have the need to be able to take your dog regularly to public places for practice. To earn this access, you must show the public you can be trusted.

Generally, the bills for building and maintenance of public places are paid by people with purposes that have nothing to do with our dogs. Handlers who wish to be welcome there with dogs must respect the purpose of each place. If it's a place of business, for example, handlers whose dogs interfere with customers or employees trying to do business will be asked to leave.

If your dog is entitled to wear identification from a particular therapy dog organization, it's a good idea to put it on the dog when you go out in public. If all handlers do this, the public will learn what a therapy dog is. It also lets people know that this dog, unlike a dog assisting a disabled person, can be petted when working in public.

When out practicing, you will encounter people who can benefit from the therapy dog. Take time for them; that's what being a therapy dog handler is all about.

7.7. TRAINING IN PUBLIC

Therapy dog handlers work their dogs on control commands in public a great deal. If you took your dog through an obedience class, or if you're naturally rather gruff with your dog, you may need to learn a new style of handling. It's standard in much training to use a firm command tone. The rules of obedience competition say not to command your dog harshly in the ring, but people do. On group Stays in the ring, I always had to wait until the other handlers had commanded their dogs in thundering tones before there was a quiet instant for me to give my dog the pleasant-voiced command to which it was trained. I trained my dogs like this because my goal was to walk with them in the neighborhood. I didn't want to roar commands in the street. I wanted my dogs to obey polite commands and handling.

Besides the way it looks in public, there is another reason to train your dog to a courteous command tone. If you want your voice to have the full range of meaning for your dog that it can have, you need to teach the dog to obey commands given in a pleasant tone. Increasing the toughness in your tone will then have meaning. If you yell, snarl or growl your commands in the first place, you've used up all the power of your voice and will have to resort to other means when your dog fails to obey a command. You'd have a hard time developing skills for therapy dog work.

Obedience classes often stress correcting the dog with a collar jerk every time it makes a mistake. This promotes precise responses to commands. Handlers aren't allowed to correct dogs in the ring, but some trainers feel this should be the only time the dog doesn't get corrected. This philosophy doesn't work when training and handling therapy dogs in public.

The way you handle your dog will determine people's opinions of you and your dog. If you treat the dog with obvious love and respect, they will think better of you both, trust you and be more willing to accept your presence in a public place. Also, people tend to treat your dog the way you do. Your kindness toward the dog becomes a model for them. I've seen this many times, but one of the most touching took me by surprise. On a nursing home visit, an elderly lady had invited little Angel to stand on hind legs for petting. When she finished petting Angel, the lady gently lowered her front legs to the ground, just as I do. I do it to reduce joint stress and the risk of arthritis as the dog ages. I had never said anything about it; I just always do it. This kind lady's action showed me how much she cared about Angel and me.

Here are some principles for training with your dog in public which you may care to review:

1. Use a pleasant tone of voice in addressing your dog. Don't use a ''mean'' tone.
2. Make corrections fast and brief. Come out praising the next instant.
3. Don't use ''lay in wait'' tactics when training in public. Instead, work closely with the dog and teach it that it isn't going to be allowed to start the misbehavior. Don't, for example, let your dog lunge at, and possibly traumatize, another person or dog so you can correct it.

    Interrupting misbehavior early has three benefits besides being more acceptable in public. Earlier intervention is more likely to teach the dog to control and redirect its own impulses. Second, it avoids correcting a dog in the act of attacking, which can increase the dog's dislike of the intended victim and make the dog more eager to attack the next time. Third, violence begets violence: tough correction can turn your dog into a bully. This treatment from parents turns children into bullies, and into adults who may abuse their own children. Just as with children, the dog you have overcorrected may never try to defy you, but may instead try it with weaker humans, especially children.

Earlier interventions don't require violent corrections and don't risk this accidental teaching of aggression. If you think you must set up and correct a dog for aggressive behavior, do it in private with the informed consent of the target. Be cautious about working such a dog in public or considering it for therapy dog work.

4. Don't go into a shop and leave the dog out of your sight on a Stay outside. It's not fair to the dog, to other people or to their dogs. Stay where you can see your dog, and don't even move away from the dog on Stays in public until you know the dog is reliable.

5. Praise at least ten times as much as you correct—and say it like you mean it.

6. When in public, work on things the dog does well and enjoys. Concentrate on teaching the dog what to do, rather than what not to do.

7. Beware of burnout. Find sources of inspiration, and continually work to improve your skills. Don't work the dog, especially in public, when you can't muster up a happy mood and a positive attitude.

8. Take time to talk to people who approach you with questions. Consider this your ''rent'' for training in public places. If you don't have time for people, train in private that day.

9. Read books about training for dogs that guide the blind. These trainers work regularly in public, too, and like therapy dog handlers, they train dogs for the real world. The main difference is that therapy dogs learn to interact with strangers, while dogs that guide the blind must learn to ignore strangers when working.

10. Listen to comments people make when watching you with your dog in public, especially those they don't mean for you to hear. Some are nonsense, but sometimes people see

things you don't see. Often it will be inappropriate for you to say anything, but think it over later.

A good trainer is always evaluating him- or herself, admitting mistakes and working to improve. It's far too easy to form the habit of blaming the dog, or blaming other people.

Practicing social skills in public is not only necessary for a therapy dog and handler, but it's also fun! When you become proficient at working your dog in public with skill and courtesy, the two of you are ready for therapy dog visits.

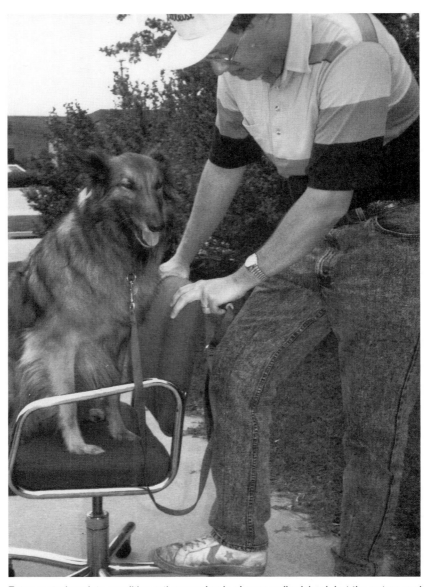

Extra control work to condition a therapy dog is always well advised, but the nature and degree depend on the dog's individual temperament and what is needed to maintain complete control when the dog is on a therapy visit. The trainer's ability to simulate the stresses and conditions the dog will face also have an important bearing on its poise at work.

8

Extra Control Work

THE CHAPTER on basic control covered skills needed before working a dog in public. The point at which a dog is ready for that will vary widely. All my dogs did much of their basic training on the streets in the neighborhood. However, many owners and dogs will need complete command work—and perhaps extra work—before venturing out. It depends on the sort of mischief your partly trained dog wants to get into, and how easily you can control the dog. As you teach your dog extra commands, you gain more options for control, which is necessary for some dogs.

Besides improving basic control, there are several good reasons to learn extra control work with your therapy dog. Learning new skills will keep work lively and interesting for both you and the dog. Earlier work will improve as you learn new things. You will be able to help people more fully on therapy dog visits and your relationship with your dog will deepen. You and your dog will become a smoother and better team.

It's impossible to cover every trained behavior that might be useful for a therapy dog and handler. Dogs, handlers and facilities are all different, with different needs. Beyond basic control work, therapy dogs and their handlers won't learn—or need to learn—all the same things.

It's been said that you can't remain in one place—you're always either moving forward or moving backward. This is certainly true of dog training skill, for both dog and handler. I hope this chapter will propel you forward, and inspire you to keep progressing for as long as you work with therapy dogs.

8.1. SIGNALS

One of the most useful skills you can teach your dog is to respond to commands given by signal. In a way, the dog finds signals easier than words, because signals are more like a dog's own, non-verbal language.

As a beginning dog trainer, I remember poring over pictures in dog books and asking other trainers for signals to teach my dogs. Some told me that you can use anything you want as a signal. That's true, but it's also true that I often tried several different signals before finding one that worked well for me. So I'll tell you some of my signals. Realize that you are free to make up your own, or borrow from others until you find signals you like. As with tone of voice, experiment with your signals to learn what communicates best with your dog.

Sit

I have two signals for Sit. One is done up close, the other at a distance. When the dog is near me, I use the right hand, palm upward, fingers extended and together. My wrist may be held straight or I may bend the hand at the wrist, depending on how close to the dog I am. The motion brings the hand sharply upward.

The farther the hand travels, the more emphatic the signal. As you and your dog progress, you'll use less movement, and when you do use a bigger signal, your dog will respond the same way as to the difference between a soft voice and a louder voice on a verbal command. This aids in controlling your dog when it's distracted.

For my Sit signal from a distance, I use the left arm. The palm faces the dog to start, and the hand travels to the front, rotates to the highest point over my head and backwards to my side through a continuous circle—it starts at my side and circles front, up, back and down to my side.

I developed this signal to use in the competition ring on the signal exercise, and I still like it. Do the movement as fast as you

The "Sit" signal.

The "Sit" signal at a distance. Bill's arm rotates front, up, over, back and drops to his side.

"Down" signal at a distance. Bill's arm starts from his side, rotates back, up, over, front and drops to his side.

can because dogs notice and see movement far better than they see a motionless object, so holding your signal after you've started it doesn't help as much as doing the signal fast. Make sure your arm shows to the side and isn't, from the dog's point of view, blocked by your body.

Most dogs have a wide range of side vision and may see a signal even with their heads turned. However, in therapy dog work you should get the dog's attention before giving it a signal, since the dog is supposed to be looking at other people rather than at the handler. The dog can learn to come to attention on its name, when you snap your fingers, clap your hands, slap your thigh or any number of other sounds. You can also wave a hand to catch the dog's eye, or touch the dog lightly.

Avoid moving your shoulders, head or other part of your body when teaching your dog a hand signal. Other movements can easily become a part of your signal to your dog—unbeknownst to you! A mirror or store window can help you check yourself.

Down

My Down signal also depends on the dog's distance from me. The Down signal is given with the palm downward. To Down a dog that's near me, I use the first two fingers. I lean over and hold the first two fingers of my right hand in front of the dog's nose, and draw them down to the floor for the dog's nose to follow as it goes Down. This is a clear and gentle signal that elicits obedience from a cooperative dog. I saw the power of this signal at an obedience event when another handler came to me and asked what to do if her dog refused to lie down in the ring—which he was doing right then in practice. I showed her my signal, and minutes later in the ring, her dog obeyed it!

My Down signal from a distance is similar to the Sit. I use the right arm for the Down. I do this because I first teach the signals at a distance in a standard order: Down, Sit, then Come. Alternating arms—always using the right arm for Down, the left for Sit, and the right for Come—lets my dog distinguish the signals easily. Later I also vary the order and use the signals in other situations to broaden the dog's training. Like the Sit, the Down signal starts at my side, this time with the palm facing away from the dog. I rotate the arm back, up, front and down to my side.

One thing I especially like about these signals is that, unlike such commonly used signals as raising one arm up and back down, I don't move my arm through a full rotation by accident when working my dog. If I straighten my glasses or hair, it won't look to my dog like a signal.

A good way to teach a signal when the dog already knows a command word is to first give the signal and then say the word. The dog will learn that the word is going to come after that signal, and will anticipate the verbal command by responding to the signal. You can then drop the word. When the dog doesn't see or fails to obey the signal, you can use the word as a mild correction. You might say "No," or you might use another sound, such as "Uh-oh!" when the dog misses the signal, then follow with the word, a repeat of the signal or both together. If you think the dog deliberately disobeyed, walk to the dog and put its body through the motion of the command.

Though in therapy dog handling you will alert your dog before giving a signal, you can teach the dog to focus attention as a useful training exercise. I like to train until the dog will watch me for up to fifteen seconds between signals. Be sure to vary the intervals, so the dog will obey no matter what the time between commands. Dogs have an acute sense of time and will sometimes learn to do that action at that time interval even without a command, unless you vary the interval to avoid setting such a pattern.

You don't want the dog to anticipate and do the next position without your signal. This need not be a big problem. Whenever the dog makes this mistake, say "No," put the dog back into the previous position, and have it wait for your signal. Sometimes don't give the signal your dog expects—give a different one, or a release. Up to sixty feet is a good distance to aim for with signals, building distance gradually. As your dog ages, signals can help you check its vision!

Heel

Another signal you may want to teach your dog is one for Heel. Many dogs learn to take as a signal the movement of your left foot, or knee, if you always start on the left foot when you give the Heel command. If you want to pattern the dog this way, start on the right foot whenever you leave the dog to Stay.

For my Heel signal, I turn the palm of my left hand toward my leg, hold the fingers straight and together, and move the hand forward, then back to my side.

162

The "Come" signal. Bill's arm goes out to his side, level with his shoulder, then in to his chest with the beckoning motion shown here.

The "Go-Out" signal also works to cast the dog out for a retrieve or a greeting.

The signal Bill is giving Star here gives her a line to the specific object to be retrieved.

163

You can also give the Heel signal with the dog starting from several feet behind you. This is useful in teaching Heel position.

Come

The Come signal is important, and fairly easy. Most handlers use the same one. It's given with the right arm, although like most signals, the dog will understand it almost as easily if for some reason you have to change hands.

The C signal has your right arm move out to the side, to an extended position level with your shoulder, palm toward the dog. Without pausing, bring the hand sharply across your chest, palm inward now, in a beckoning motion. Then the hand drops back to your side.

Go Out, Take It, Go Say "Hi"!

Other useful signals include the Go Out, which is a gesture I do with the right hand, extending the first two fingers and moving my hand from the dog's head forward. It means for the dog to move away from me. The signal for the retrieve can be the same, or you can use the left arm shooting forward from your side. These are vigorous signals, meant to cast the dog outward.

A stationary signal to give your dog a precise line to a retrieve or to greet a specific person works best if you hold your forearm and hand in a straight line above the dog's head (the palm of your hand vertical, not horizontal), just between its eyes. This is clearer to the dog than a signal at the side of the head. Try it on your own head, and you'll see that your hand at the side of your head gives an unclear direction.

Paws Up

Another useful signal and command for the therapy dog is Paws Up. This transfers to anything you want the dog to put front feet on—pat the object and say "Paws up."

I teach my big dogs this as a redirected desire to jump on me. I hold my forearm out and have the dog put its front feet there, for a greeting and as a reward for good work. This is the only way I want big dogs to jump on me—I don't want them jumping on my front and damaging clothing.

"Paws Up."

"Paws Up" to the arm of a desk chair helps prepare the dog to safely greet an occupant of a wheelchair.

The safest way for a therapy dog to accept a treat is from an open hand — even if it's also the wettest way!

Tossing a treat can result in a fall or injury even in a well-conditioned, athletic dog.

166

Paws Up is ideal for getting a therapy dog's paws to the arm of a wheelchair or the edge of a bed so a person with limited mobility can pet the dog. You can easily teach the dog the difference between Paws Up—just the front feet to the spot you pat—and Come Up, when you need the whole dog on that spot.

8.2. TREATS

Teaching your dog to accept treats safely from other people is an extra skill, because you don't have to allow others to feed your dog on visits—I choose not to. But treats can be used to advantage, with precautions.

One problem with treats is that people may give the dog something harmful. People have been known to feed their medications to therapy dogs. I recommend that you bring the treats yourself and teach the dog not to accept food on visits from anyone's hand without your permission. In training, don't allow the dog to get the treat until you say it may.

Another serious problem is the dog that snatches at food could hurt someone's fingers. Broken skin from a dog's teeth, even when the dog intended no harm, will likely be considered a dog bite from a Health Department standpoint.

There are three ways to give such a dog a treat without thorough training, but all have drawbacks.

You can hold the treat in the palm of your hand. The hand will get slobbery, but the dog will probably take the treat gently, because snapping won't work.

You can toss the treat to the dog. This can result in the dog lunging unpredictably to catch it, and possibly injuring itself or someone else.

The third method, if the treat-snapping dog knows good Stays, is to put the dog on a Stay command, set the treat down and release the dog to take it. This isn't effective for letting a person in a facility attract the dog's attention by giving it food. Since that is the major use of treats with therapy dogs on visits, you really should train the dog to accept treats properly and straight from the person, if you intend to let people give it treats on visits.

The solution to treat-snapping is to teach the dog to take food gently from fingers, which is the way most people will offer it. Teach this by not releasing the treat until the dog takes it correctly,

The proper use of treats is an excellent training device for a therapy dog. Many handlers train their dogs to accept treats only on the proper signal. Here Bill Davis sets out a tempting morsel in front of Star as she holds a firm "Stay."

The cue she was waiting for—when Bill said "Okay!" he released Star to collect her reward.

To teach a dog to take a treat gently, keep your hand closed around it while showing the dog that it's there. The dog will show when it's ready to take the treat gently.

168

with the teeth not touching your skin. You should feel only soft lips and tongue.

One concern I have about treats is the risk of giving people the idea that therapy dogs only respond to people for food. Too many people already believe this. For a dog that enjoys interacting with people, the food may even get in the way. We should work therapy dogs on their social instincts and let people see that the dogs enjoy interacting with people.

Ask hunting dog trainers, herding dog trainers or police dog trainers what they think of teaching dogs to do those jobs by using food treats. They'll tell you that the dog should have the right instincts for the job in the first place, and should learn to work to please the handler and for the satisfaction of expressing its instincts. The best therapy dogs will have strong social drives and will desire to please their handlers. They will interact with friendly strangers in partnership with their handlers. Food should not be necessary.

Giving food to the dog can be meaningful to some of the people therapy dogs work with, and has been known to produce good results. If you work with food, be sure your dog knows how to accept food properly, yet will also work without food.

8.3. GREETINGS: SHAKE HANDS, KISS

Two extra skills your therapy dog can use to good advantage are greetings: shaking hands and kissing. These are in addition to the basic greeting of the dog approaching a person and offering its head for petting.

I don't recommend forcing a dog to learn either of these behaviors. Just encourage whatever natural inclination the dog shows, and use a word for the behavior so that over time the dog will learn what you mean when you say "Shake hands," "Kiss" or whatever cue words you decide to use.

Shaking hands is a submissive gesture from the dog, so teach it gently. Support the paw without squeezing it, and don't grab the foot or refuse to let go. The bones in a dog's foot are small. Monitor other people when your dog shakes hands with them to protect the dog from harm. Gradually, through play, you can build your dog's tolerance for less-gentle handling of the feet, in case someone does latch on too hard.

I thought at first that people wouldn't like to be licked by a

Shaking hands is an attractive behavior, easy to teach, easy to learn and a good ice-breaking skill for the well-trained therapy dog.

The happiness a therapy dog brings by simply licking someone's hand is plainly evident on the face of the lady being charmed by Angel.

therapy dog, but I was wrong. Many people love it, and it stimulates them in positive ways. Therefore, I suggest that you teach the dog when to stop licking by gently pulling the dog back when enough is enough. When you want your dog to stop licking you, pull away, or hold the dog's head back gently with your hand. A rough correction might stop the dog from ever licking again, losing a behavior in your dog that can help people.

The submissive, solicitous-toward-people attitude that prompts a dog to lick should be encouraged. Shaking hands is an attractive behavior that will break the ice when you and your dog meet new people. These are good skills for a therapy dog to have.

8.4. WALKING SKILLS

For walking in public as well as on visits, you may want to teach your dog three walking behaviors not used in basic control training. These behaviors are also used in other dog jobs.

The first of these special commands is Wait, which tells the dog to stop but remain alert for your next command. Some trainers use this to signify a Stay but I prefer to allow the dog to change body position on Wait, as long as it stays in one spot. Of course you can teach your dog both, using different words. I let the dog change position on Wait because I use it on therapy dog visits and on walks when I want the dog to feel free to sit or lie down if we stop for a long time and it gets tired.

A second walking cue is whether or not you want the dog to pull. If your dog pulls a racing sled or dog cart, you'll learn a specific command from that work. I say "Go-go!" with extra zest if I want to encourage pulling.

When I don't want the dog to pull, but I do want it to continue moving forward, I say "Easy." This word also works the dog through a situation in which you want it to move gently and carefully, and to take further cues from you. Among other things, I use Easy to steer a dog through broken glass when out walking.

8.5. POSITIONS IN PLACE

Every large therapy dog that looks intimidating should learn positions in place. This uses words and signals for Sit, Down and

The Front position.

Stand. When you meet someone who's afraid of your dog, stay back out of the range that would panic that person. Remaining in one spot, give the dog pleasant verbal commands and gentle but noticeable signals for the positions, in any order you wish. This sequence relaxes people by showing that your dog is under control.

Teach this gently. It's a powerful exercise that can make a dog feel quite oppressed if you overdo it. Most of the time when you give your dog a command, there should be a reason for it, if you wish to preserve the quality of initiative in your dog. If you drill your dog too much, you will destroy its initiative. Do it just enough to instill good discipline, and season it liberally with praise.

8.6. FRONT, FINISH, MOVE, BACK

The Front position, dog and handler facing one another with the dog seated, is useful when lining your dog up for petting. It's easy to make a dog go sour on its work by teaching Fronts too harshly. Don't grab at the dog or use the leash to yank the dog into a straight Front. You want the dog to come to you happily, and never to experience anything unpleasant when it does.

The Finish is a refinement of the Heel position. From sitting in Front position, the dog can come to Heel either by turning 180 degrees counterclockwise and stopping seated at your left; or by going around your right side, behind you, and to your left. These are taught using careful footwork and guiding the dog with the leash.

I teach the Finish exercises to my dogs gently, and I prefer that each dog learn both, for maximum maneuverability on therapy dog visits. These exercises were intended to be done with the dog starting from Front, but they are extremely useful to bring a dog to Heel from walking ahead of you as well. Working on Finishes is useful polish and will improve your skill with the leash.

The footwork for the Finish with the dog coming to your left and either pivoting or leaping (the dog's personal style will determine which) 180 degrees counterclockwise starts by stepping back with your left foot. While guiding the dog with the leash in your left hand, you're teaching the dog a signal with that hand.

As the dog turns toward you, step forward to your original position, letting the dog follow the movement of your left foot.

The around-behind Finish requires you to start with the leash in your right hand—the foundation for a signal. Step back with your

Star demonstrates the results of Michael Tucker's gentle method for teaching the around-behind Finish. To start, Star sits Front, then Bill moves his right foot to her right side.

Bill moves his left foot forward and stands squarely beside Star.

"Star, Heel!" As your dog learns what you want, reduce, then eliminate the foot movements. This technique is fun, it presents no threat to the dog and, most important, it works!

right foot. Guide the dog around behind you (starting to your right), change the leash behind your back to your left hand and step forward with your left foot. As you stop in your original position you want the dog to Sit at Heel. Over time, drop the foot movement and give the signal and verbal command simultaneously.

There are other ways to teach these exercises. For a larger dog, you may need to travel two steps backward to give the dog room to turn. An excellent alternative method for the around-behind Finish comes from Michael Tucker's book *Dog Training Made Easy* (New York: Howell Book House, 1990). Starting with the dog in Front position, step forward and stand at your seated dog's right. Then twist your upper body left and backward to look under your left arm and encourage the dog to travel around you to Heel. Gradually move less and less until the dog does all the traveling.

Two typical Finish commands are Heel and Swing, but feel free to make up your own. Other useful commands are Move and Back. Move alerts the dog to notice you and to get out of your way. When you want the dog to let you step over it instead of moving out of your way, say "Stay" or "Wait," instead of leaving the dog to guess and yourself perhaps to trip! "Back" helps the dog learn to back up, which dogs don't do very well without practice. Be gentle, and help the dog with your hands. It's good for the dog to learn a new way of moving, and it gives you another option for maneuvering on therapy dog visits.

8.7. LANGUAGE

In everything you do with your dog, language plays a part. The more words your dog knows, the better. Don't make teaching new words drudgery; do it as a natural part of relating to your dog.

Continuous verbal encouragement ("Good dog! You can do it!") can be a strong motivator for your dog and can help your work. However, until your dog becomes accustomed to your free flow of conversation, especially while working, you will not be able to use this technique. Instead of encouraging the dog, your voice will distract it. Don't use the dog's command name during verbal encouragement. Use a nickname, or no name, so the dog will not think you are giving a new command. Verbal encouragement helps keep the dog working on a command you have already given.

It may be useful for you to teach your dog commands in a

foreign language, or secret cues that only you and the dog understand. Sometimes you may want to conceal your cues. I find on therapy dog visits that some people enjoy being with the dog with little involvement from me. This is a major reason to teach the dog signals. I can use subtle cues to remain in control yet not intrude on the interaction.

Some competitive obedience handlers don't use the dog's name before any command. Others instruct students to use the name only when commanding the dog to move. They say never to use the name if the command will be Stay, for example, because the dog might move when it hears its name.

I usually use the dog's name with any command, for two reasons:

1. I talk to my dogs a lot and frequently use verbal encouragement. In order for this not to be a distraction, and so the dog can distinguish a command from other talk, I preface a command with the dog's name.
2. My dogs are together except when I take one out to work. In order to have good control of a pack of dogs, I need to say which dog I'm commanding. By using names with commands, I can command three dogs to do three different things.

Another reason for using the dog's name with a command is something I did intuitively before I realized why. When I want the dog to do a command action, but it is not a command (such as on the veterinarian's examining table), I can use the name after the command word. This is a weaker form of addressing the dog, which is why we normally use the dog's name before any command: "Saint, Come!" not "Come, Saint!" Saint will alert to his name and respond more accurately if the name comes first—he'll be more likely to hear the command word. This technique also works with husbands!

When I want to give the dog some latitude about the command word, I don't use the command name first. I change my voice tone, and I physically assist the dog to do the action. I may also add extra words to the command ("Star, can you sit?"), or repeat it like a chant. Dogs easily learn these differences.

Make it a habit to use positive language with your dog. This will give you a more positive attitude toward the dog and will make the right impression when working your dog in public. A positive name for your dog is also important, and positive nicknames: Handsome, not Ugly; Clever Girl, not Dumb Dog.

Experiment with ways to get your dog to do new things. When working in a new situation, use your voice and body language to see if you can communicate to your dog how to do what you wish. This is fun and and great learning experience for both of you. Do these activities in a spirit of play, and don't correct the dog for failing to understand. By rewarding the dog for trying, you build in your dog the important quality of persisting in a task. At the same time, you expand your handling skills and your dog's education.

Another important aspect of language is how you use the word "no." Some trainers say not to use it at all. I use it a lot, with various meanings. A roared *"No!!!"* is a severe correction that stops my dogs in their tracks. This is an emergency word when used in a tough tone, not to be thrown around carelessly. If you were to do that, you would devalue the word until it no longer worked in an emergency, and you might cow the dog. The tone changes the word. For "not now," I say a soft "no," or "no-no." For "That was the wrong choice; try again," I say "no-o-o-o," in a voice that draws the word out into almost a question at the end.

To get a fast response from your dog, say a command quickly—but clearly, and the same way every time. It doesn't need to be loud, but short and clipped, or "staccato." Another musical term that applies to dog training is "dynamics"—varying the volume to vary the meaning. Musical people make good dog trainers.

You can use tones to "orient" your dog. You might say something like "Ih!" or "Hey!" to get your dog to stop what it's doing and look to you for instructions. These should come from your gut—use your diaphragm to force the sound sharply out.

8.8. DOES YOUR THERAPY DOG NEED A HOBBY?

Some dogs have so much energy that they're unlikely to make good house dogs without an outlet. Some high-energy dogs need time to mature, perhaps even several years, before having the necessary composure to serve as therapy dogs. These dogs need other activities. People we visit enjoy all kinds of dogs, and if the dogs have had colorful careers, all the better.

Most of the activities people pursue passionately with their dogs can also be done casually, for fun, without interfering with therapy dog visits. If you choose to do this, make sure the instructor and other participants understand and support your priorities.

8.9. TRICKS

Should your therapy dog do tricks? This is up to you. Tricks are fun and easy to teach the dog, when done with a playful attitude. Many tricks teach useful skills, and entertainment can be therapeutic. However, a therapy dog visit should consist primarily of interaction between the dog and people. An overemphasis on tricks is a problem in therapy dog work. It steals time away from interaction with people, focuses training on tricks instead of more important skills and discourages good volunteers. It's unwise to use therapy dog visits as an opportunity to practice or train a dog for competitive obedience events. The corrections necessary to make a dog work precisely are unacceptable on therapy dog visits. The working conditions on visits could actually harm your dog's performance in competition.

However, if what you really want to do is perform with your dog, go for it. But never discourage other handlers who want to do therapy dog visits without performing.

What tricks can you use? You might be surprised at what becomes a trick if the dog will do it on cue and under control. Catching, fetching, demonstrating basic obedience exercises and controlled playing with your dog will all work. The book *Dog Tricks* by Benjamin and Haggerty (New York: Howell Book House, 1982) includes many ideas. Pick things that interest you and won't hurt the dog. Not all dogs have the instincts or physiques for all tricks. The fewer and lighter your props, the better. It's usually not worth the effort to bring jumps, since most surfaces will be unsafe for jumping anyway.

A good therapy dog watches carefully for people moving around when performing on a visit, to avoid running into anyone. That will take the edge off the very showy, "fired from a gun" response that wins in the ring. This intense performance could be dangerous to individuals in a nursing home or other facility, unless the performance area is kept completely clear of people.

Remember that you and your dog aren't judged on precision when performing on therapy dog visits. If it doesn't go well, give the dog one more try, helping so much that it can't fail. If you don't know how to do this, you aren't ready to perform in this setting; in the chaos of a facility, the dog will make mistakes. The people will often applaud enthusiastically for a successful second try. If the second try fails, go on to something else. You're there to serve the needs of the people in the facility, not to train your dog to perform.

There's no cause to feel self-conscious when doing a demonstration with your dog in front of a group. Just keep your mind on your dog. The people couldn't watch you if they tried—all eyes are magnetically drawn to the dog. You'll feel far less nervous as you gain experience.

Whenever possible, I ask the media to show interaction between people and dogs, not tricks. Photographs of these people are good for them, building self-esteem and giving other benefits. If television coverage of a therapy dog visit emphasizes tricks, it misses the chance to do something therapeutic for the people in the facility by featuring them on television.

A faithful volunteer with a well-behaved dog that does no tricks at all is just as important in therapy dog work as the flashiest performer. In fact, those who don't do tricks often do better therapy.

How well a dog performs training routines in a facility is often less important than the interaction that takes place between the dog and those it visits. The rapport that exists between your therapy dog and you is the real key that will unlock a multitude of doors.

Good handling is the essential ingredient in good therapy dog work. A capable handler with a confident dog make all benefits possible from good therapy work gratifying realities.

9

The Handler's Job

THE KEY to successful therapy dog work is the handler. The lack of good handling can be an insurmountable handicap for even the best of therapy dogs. With the right handler, a dog that's initially acceptable as a therapy dog improves over time on the job. With the right handler, the dog gets the proper care to stay in service as long as possible. In addition, the correct decisions get made about which facilities a dog should serve and when the dog is healthy enough for work. Everyone benefits.

Like the dogs, therapy dog handlers can learn much of the job. A strong desire to do this work is necessary, because it takes commitment. A few personality traits may help, such as being a meticulously careful person. However, successful therapy dog handlers have all sorts of personalities. Desire, well-guided effort and a reasonably well-suited dog can prepare most good dog handlers to do therapy dog work. It's the handler that the public and the facilities look to. If they don't trust you, they won't trust your dog, no matter how great the dog is. If they do trust you, they'll soon trust your dog.

9.1. ATTITUDE

Years in business taught me a valuable lesson for therapy dog work: attitude. Any job that involves dealing with the public requires a good attitude. Even police officers do most of their work by persuading people, rather than by using authority or force. In all dealings with people, therapy dog handlers need to have remarkably good attitudes. Any dog trainer will tell you not to work your dog when you're in a bad mood. This goes double for working a therapy dog around people.

Here are some techniques I use to maintain a good attitude:

1. *Control the schedule.* I find that more than two visits per week or eight visits per month are too many for me. To keep a good attitude, I keep the level of visits on the schedule to a point that keeps me mentally and emotionally ready, not tired or burned out. If one visit a month is all you have time to do, do that one faithfully and know that you will be far more effective than someone who overschedules, doesn't keep commitments and quits.

2. *Get yourself into a good mood on the way to the visit.* I have a cassette player in the car that I sing along with as I drive. This also warms up my voice and sharpens my timing for working the dog.

   It's important to get a smile on by the time you walk in the door. Working on your mood is not fake. It will actually improve the way you feel. Acting as if you're happy helps you feel happy. Practice will help your ability to do this. Try to get enough sleep the night before. Have a meal or snack before the visit, on a schedule that will give you stable blood sugar (do the same for your dog). Allow yourself plenty of time to get ready and to make the trip, so you won't arrive late and flustered. If you're late, apologize and then forget it—don't let it ruin the rest of the visit.

3. *Put other things out of your mind and concentrate on your job.* Remember that it would only take a second for someone to fall because of your dog, or to hurt your dog and perhaps terrify it into biting. You can't afford to be inattentive. Understanding this may help you realize that you simply can't afford to indulge in a bad mood during a visit.

I invariably find that no matter how I feel when I start, I'm in a good mood by the end of the visit. It's a blessing when other things in my life aren't going well. It's a time to forget my worries and focus on the dog and the people I'm there to help. The worries are lighter when next I think of them.

If there's nothing you can do to control your feelings, you'll need to cancel that visit. It's unsafe to do a therapy dog visit when you're not in the right mental state to control your dog. Practice can improve your ability to control moods. If you find you can't control your emotions, therapy dog handling is not the volunteer job for you.

9.2. BE READY TO SAY NO

One job that sometimes only the handler is in a position to do is to say no. There are at least four things the handler must be ready to say no to:

1. *Be ready to say no to your dog becoming a therapy dog, or continuing to work as one.* If you feel that your dog wouldn't enjoy therapy dog work, or if you don't feel comfortable handling that dog on visits, your feelings are valid. Don't let anyone talk you into acting against your doubt. If you have a strong desire to do this work, explore your feelings until you discover what's causing your doubt. There may be a way to work it out. Lots of people are willing to help you.

    You know your dog better than its veterinarian does, or than any dog trainer or instructor could know it. Sometimes an obedience class instructor may consider a dog okay when the handler doesn't. When in obedience class the instructor is in charge and ready to back you, but on therapy dog visits the tough corrections common in obedience classes are unacceptable. The obedience instructor may have little or no experience with therapy dog work—doing therapy dog visits and also instructing obedience classes is a lot to ask of anyone! On therapy dog visits, there's much less room for mistakes than in class. Listen to your doubts.

    Your veterinarian listens intently to your "feelings" about your dog. What seem like feelings or hunches are often people's perceptions of the dog's nonverbal language. The dog has, in its way, *told* you how it feels. You may not be able to put this knowledge into words, because it doesn't come to you in words. This information is vital, and you must respect it. If you don't feel confident that your dog is ready to be a therapy dog, say no.

2. *Be ready to say no to a particular visit.* Your dog may not be feeling well enough to do a visit, without definite symptoms. No dog should be taken on a therapy dog visit when it's ill. This is unfair to the dog and could result in an irritable or sore dog injuring someone, even though that is completely uncharacteristic behavior for that dog.

   I learned this lesson from one of my own dogs. Some time ago, Star was ill and in pain for about five weeks. If she even thought I was going to give her a command, she would give me a desperate look that told me she simply could not obey. Since she had been taught that a command must be obeyed, she felt cornered at the idea that I might tell her to do something that she couldn't do.

   During Star's illness, little Angel went up to Star on the bed and made play motions to her face. Star cried with a pitiful wail to tell Angel she couldn't play. I'll never forget that sound. Star couldn't play hard for months, and now when I see the two pals rough-and-tumble, I feel deeply grateful for Star's total recovery. But remembering Star's illness reminds me not to take sick, injured, sore or tired dogs on therapy visits.

3. *Be ready to say no to a particular facility.* If you belong to a therapy dog group that schedules the visits for you, you may find that a facility the group is going to—or one that invites you individually to bring a dog—doesn't "feel" right for you and your dog.

   When I had only one therapy dog, small Angel, I didn't feel she should work with people who had a lot of mobility without good understanding of their actions, such as pre-school children or emotionally disturbed people. After I began working large therapy dogs on visits, I found that I had been right. My large dogs were fine with these groups, but there was too much physical pressure on the small dogs—their handlers confirmed this.

4. *Be ready to say no to something someone wants to do to your dog.* If you feel your dog shouldn't be worked by people other than you, say no. If you feel a particular person might mistreat your dog, keep your dog away from that

person. Don't let anyone "test" your therapy dog in a way you don't approve. Should a staff member or other person suggest or even order you to work your dog in a way you feel is unsafe or unfair to your dog, say no. In the instance that something goes wrong and someone gets hurt, you are held accountable and could even lose your dog. If someone traumatizes your dog, you'll be the one with the job of rehabilitating the dog. These facts put you in charge when it comes to what is to be done to your dog.

This doesn't mean to refuse to keep your dog on leash if asked, which won't harm the dog, or deprive you of exerting control and supervision. Even if you think your dog could run through the facility off leash and do no harm, you must respect the rules enforced in that situation.

What saying no *does* mean is that you have the right and the responsibility to protect your dog. It has to be you, because no one else can. This also means following your intuition concerning control of the dog. Once I had Saint at a birthday party for a friend's dog, with several strange dogs present. The hostess badgered me all day to let Saint off the leash with the other dogs, but I never did. I kept picturing one of his beautiful upright ears with a big rip in it. He spent a jolly day on leash. He still has beautiful ears.

Another time I had Star with me with other Belgian Tervurens and their owners. One of the owners urged me to let Star off the leash. I hadn't had Star long and didn't feel sure enough of her reactions to work her off leash. Her breeder jumped to my defense, telling the other dog owner that I didn't feel ready yet. Tervuren work brilliantly off leash, but owner and dog must train together to reach that level first.

When your dog is tired, thirsty, being aggravated by someone or otherwise uncomfortable or at risk, it's your job to take care of the dog.

9.3. WATER

It's vital that every therapy dog handler understand a dog's need for water. Humane treatment demands that the dog have water available. The dog's only natural means of cooling itself is by giving

Therapy work can be uncomfortably warm for the dog. The well-prepared handler will always carry water in a spray bottle for quick cool-offs and most dogs really appreciate a little "artificial sweat!"

A large dog can be intimidating to some people in facilities regardless of a gentle nature. A whimsical costume or prop helps to soften the appearance of such dogs, making them more inviting to those who need their interaction most.

Courtesy Dog Fancy Magazine

off moisture through the mouth and nose—that's why dogs pant. They don't perspire, except a little through the footpads. A dog in perfect condition shouldn't be worked in temperatures above 85 degrees. If the dog has any physical problem, the top working temperature for that dog should be lower. A typical indoor dog working on a therapy dog visit should be kept far below this top temperature limit.

Nursing homes are quite warm, because inactive people easily feel cold and are susceptible to hypothermia. Especially in summer, it may be too hot in a nursing home to ask your dog to perform. It may also be too hot, unless your car has good air-conditioning, to get the dog there safely.

Water on hand is essential for a therapy dog. If the facility you are visiting is near your home, you may be able to take in just a dish and a towel and fill the dish with the facility's water (but do bring water in your car). If the water is different from your water at home, you'll need to carry water in, because strange water can make a dog sick. The towel goes under the dish. Any spill in a facility can cause someone to slip and fall, so be fussy about wiping up. Be sure to dry any spots on the floor where your dog drools. I carry a second towel to wipe people's hands (if they wish) after the dog licks them, to place on a lap or furniture before a dog sits or lies there and for other needs. I use thick towels for good absorbency, and launder them after each visit.

Using a spray bottle, you can spritz a dog with water, especially on the head, tummy and chest (and the back, when in the sun). I call this "artificial sweat." It allows the dog to benefit from the same evaporative cooling that human perspiration provides. Using this technique, you can make your dog more comfortable and it will almost surely work better for you. However, the technique won't work in high humidity and it won't make it reasonable to work any dog in unsafe conditions.

9.4. WHAT TO WEAR

Since working a dog is a physical task, dress comfortably, but don't wear clothing that is revealing, scruffy or soiled. Therapy dog handlers do not need to dress as formally as administrative personnel in a facility; it is appropriate to dress more like those who take care of people.

I wear an identification tag on therapy dog visits, and have my dogs wear therapy dog identification. It makes sense for everyone in a facility to wear identification for security reasons. An ID tag for yourself can be a simple affair. Some office supply stores sell plastic holders about the size of a business card that will either clip or pin onto clothing. You can slip an ID card inside. For the dog, some therapy dog groups specify the identification each dog is to wear. It may be a tag on the collar, a special harness, a vest or whatever they choose. The facility will appreciate ID on the therapy dog, because it helps them explain the dog's presence. Staff members often have to tell people to remove unsuitable dogs from the premises. If the therapy dog is clearly identified, it's easier for the staff to explain that this is a special dog and handler, inside the facility by appointment.

One issue that raises controversy with handlers is costumes on dogs. Some people claim that costumes embarrass dogs. I doubt it. When a dog seems to dislike a costume, it's more likely that the costume is uncomfortable or the dog hasn't been properly introduced to it. I feel that it is necessary for my dog Saint to wear a colorful, ruffled clown collar on all therapy dog visits. It makes an enormous difference in his appearance, and keeps most people from being uncomfortable around him. It saves a lot of time that would otherwise be used to put people at ease, and it relieves people's fears. The collar is part of his uniform for visits, and I recommend that all handlers with intimidating-looking dogs consider costumes for their dogs.

A flowing or ruffled collar around the neck is a simple way to soften the dog's appearance without interfering with movement or comfort; a bandanna around the dog's neck, on the other hand, does little to make the dog look less intimidating. Other costumes may work, too, but if the costume is elaborate, don't have the dog wear it for long. Avoid costumes that make your dog hot.

9.5. TIMES OF DAY

Another part of the handler's job is to decide what time of day to do therapy dog visits, and how long visits should last. While beginners shouldn't work longer than an hour, experienced dogs and handlers may be able to do longer visits, especially in facilities they visit frequently where the dog feels at ease. You may not have a

Arrange your schedule for therapy dog visits when they will be most effective. While a good therapy dog can take advantage of a "loving session" to relax in a profferred lap, it should not be expected to work if it is tired or off its usual routine.

choice about the time of day, if a group leader does the scheduling, if the facility's schedule is restrictive or if your own schedule allows only one particular time for visits. If your own schedule is limited, you may find some facilities that can't accommodate it, but many others will. People will probably respond to your dog no matter when you come, if you come consistently and do a good job.

However, if you have the choice, I've found that weekday mornings are ideal. On weekdays, the staff is usually in full force and best able to support your visits. In the morning, people are less sleepy and less likely to be cranky than in the afternoon. The staff at facilities tell me their people are noticeably more responsive to the dogs in the mornings. Additionally, if we can reach people early, improved moods last the rest of the day—longer for some.

I also find that, at home, my dogs tend to play in the morning and sleep in the afternoon. Dogs sleep about fourteen hours a day. When we do visits in the mornings and the dogs take their regular afternoon naps, I don't find my dogs tired out by visits. They take the afternoon naps they would take anyway, and wake up with normal energy.

Many therapy dog handlers tell me their dogs are exhausted after visits. It's better to avoid that. You may also find that your dog is sluggish and works poorly when you do therapy dog visits in the afternoon. This will be even more of a problem in summer, since afternoon temperatures are the highest.

Another advantage of doing visits in the morning is that the facility's lunchtime gives you a good time to end your visit. Otherwise it can be hard to break away.

Weekend, evening and afternoon programs can all be done successfully, and one advantage can be more involvement with family members. A disadvantage is that sometimes staff has to come in on time off for weekend and evening visits.

Some facilities, such as schools, are only in session on weekdays. As therapy dog work gains recognition in communities, perhaps some employers will arrange work schedules to allow handlers to do daytime visits.

9.6. LIMITS

How much a dog is allowed to work should be carefully limited, and this, too, is the handler's job. It falls on you because no one else can know the dog well enough—or control its other activities—to make the needed decisions. The settings where the dog works, the other things the dog does besides therapy dog visits and the type of dog will all be factors.

Some therapy dog visits are quite stressful for the dog. People in facilities who aren't aware of the consequences of their actions and yet move around a lot will represent a great challenge to both handler and dog. If the people sometimes become violent, the situation can become dangerous and the dog will be aware of that. Sometimes you can predict the difficult visits, and sometimes they come unexpectedly. Select carefully where you are and where you are not willing to do therapy dog work. In my own work, I do not visit violent people. Whenever you do stressful visits, do fewer and shorter visits than you would otherwise.

Another factor is how familiar the dog is with the setting. It might be feasible to take your dog to the same facility with you five days a week, with the dog spending most of each day resting in a place where it will not be disturbed. For some dogs this would be far too much, but for others it wouldn't, especially if you give the dog good support when it works with people. The dog should always have a handler when working.

The dog will also experience less stress on one-dog visits than on visits with other dogs. The more other dogs there, and the more that are strange to your dog, the more stress. Groups need to limit how many dogs go together on a visit. Six to twelve dogs are plenty for most situations.

Small dogs have less stamina than large dogs. They generally should work for shorter periods of time and with fewer people than large dogs.

A major factor in how much a dog should work as a therapy dog is the dog's genetic makeup for work. The herding dogs have been called the workaholics of the dog world, due to their ability to remain alert and moving for long periods of time when controlling livestock. Many sporting breeds have stamina to hunt for a long day in the field. If your dog is almost too much dog at home, needing things to do to keep it from driving you bonkers, that's a dog that—with good control from you—may be able to do more therapy dog work.

Each handler must decide how much his or her dog should work. Whenever you feel a visit may have pushed your dog too hard, give the dog at least a two-week break from therapy dog visits, and during the break give the dog happy outings. Do this before the dog shows any sign of burnout and before you have committed to many visits.

9.7. ATTENTION ON DOG, POTENTIAL INJURIES

As a handler, it's your job to pay total attention to your dog when on a therapy dog visit. If you have not yet trained a dog, you will find this skill takes time for you to develop. The first night of any beginning obedience class is scary, because the handlers don't pay attention to their dogs. Eventually trainers learn, with practice, but you always have to discipline your mind to do it.

I think of this skill as like driving a car. You can't watch every part of the road at all times, but you develop habits such as checking both ways before turning left or crossing an intersection, scanning the road ahead both near and far, keeping your eyes on the stoplight while stopped waiting for it to change, checking your speed at intervals and poising your foot over the brake when passing near a child on a bicycle. The handler's habits when handling a dog are similar. Just as inattention when driving can cause an accident, inattention when handling a dog around people might result in an injury. The main reason some handlers don't pay enough attention to their dogs is that they don't understand what could go wrong.

It's a twofold responsibility—controlling the dog and protecting the dog. When working with certain people, protecting the dog will take the forefront. When working a small dog, this responsibility takes most of the handler's attention. However, a major means of protecting your dog is to use training to control the dog—to see trouble coming and to dodge it. Controlling the dog and protecting the dog go together.

If your dog is easygoing or highly trained, it may be tempting for you to let the dog work on its own with little of your attention. This would be a mistake. The dog doesn't understand the hazards, nor do the people. Only a skilled handler can manage the dog to keep everyone safe. With a dog that—either through breeding or through training—is easy to handle, the handler may not appear to work hard physically. But mentally that handler must always be at work, ready to use perhaps just a quiet word to guide the dog to safety.

The best way to explain what the handler needs to do to exert control is to give examples of what could go wrong, and how the handler might avoid or deal with each situation.

The most common serious accidents resulting from dogs in facilities are falls. Falls are common accidents even without dogs around. When elderly people fall, some of them never walk again. Even if it's a staff member or other able-bodied person who falls, it can be a serious accident.

Falls usually happen when a dog is in a facility without a handler. Don't expect a dog to figure out how to stay out of the way. Some traffic patterns are incomprehensible to a dog, when you consider that staff members do all sorts of errands in the facility, sometimes pushing heavy equipment. They may be able to see well enough to avoid a standing person or a person seated in a wheelchair, but not a dog on the floor. If you have a dog in your house, you may realize how hard it can be to avoid tripping over it. Some dogs dodge better than others; little dogs try harder, and herding dogs notice movement more. It's the handler's job to watch traffic. I don't like my dog standing too near people who are walking with obvious difficulty, especially when they're just standing up from a seated position. If there is no time to move the dog, steady Stays become precious.

Another issue in protecting people from falls is whether or not to give the person the dog's leash and let him or her walk the dog alone. The person could fall over the dog, or tangle in the leash and fall. Besides this, the person might clench up on the leash, step on the dog or otherwise mishandle the dog. Protecting the dog protects people, since a terrified dog or a dog in pain might react without thinking. If you do not feel comfortable letting others walk your dog, say no.

You can intervene when another person has the leash by grasping the leash yourself between the person's hand and the dog's collar. If the person pulls too hard, your hand can buffer pressure on the dog, and if the person needs help controlling the dog, your hand can give it.

You can read your dog's body language, especially the face, to determine if anything is upsetting the dog. A relaxed expression with the mouth open and light panting is good. I call it a relaxation response. If that isn't the dog's expression, make sure you know exactly what the people around your dog are doing. Check all sides. The dog may just be alerting to something, or it may be extremely cool, but check.

During a therapy dog visit to a facility, always be sure that your dog is safe when it is with another person. Standing or sitting, a dog could be at risk if the person it is with becomes frightened or disoriented.

Actual physical contact with the elderly should be carefully monitored. In the case of frail people an accidental scratch or bump could have real complications. A towel in the person's lap can protect both dog and human.

Courtesy Dog Fancy Magazine

Heel and Swing Finish commands will help you keep the dog out of people's way. These let you get the dog tucked up tightly at your side on a few seconds' notice. This kind of control will distinguish you as a safe handler and will be much preferred by the staff to a handler and dog that get in the way. Since people will congregate around the dog, keep hallways and other passages clear.

Another potential accident is a dog scratching a person with its toenails. This can be serious. For certain people, a scratch can be slow to heal or get infected. There could also be confusion about whether the scratch came from toenail or tooth, causing it to have to be treated as a dog bite. To guard against this injury, as well as bruises, handlers must groom their dogs' toenails. On visits, dogs shouldn't sit on people unless either clothing or other fabric (your extra towel, if needed) sufficient to prevent injury is placed between the dog's feet and the person's skin. Large dogs should not put any weight on people.

If your dog shakes hands or otherwise paws at people, monitor this behavior, and when necessary, guide the dog's foot when near a person's skin. Watch carefully that your dog doesn't step or lean on people's feet. Don't set even a small dog on a person who is extremely thin or frail.

Another potential injury may occur when there is accidental contact between the dog's teeth and someone's hands. Besides retrieving games, this can happen when people give the dog food, as discussed previously in this book. If you wish to let people feed your therapy dog on visits, be sure you do the appropriate training; or if, like me, you prefer that people don't feed your therapy dog, tell them at every opportunity. In these days of special diets, it's getting easier to persuade people that no dog is a garbage disposal. You can also tell them, if it's true, that the dog will get a treat when you return to the car. My dogs' ears perk up and they dance around when I say "Cookie!" This convinces people that I'm telling the truth, and makes them more content not to feed the dog. I also tell people that the dog has already eaten at least once that day, since I give each dog a light meal before leaving home for a therapy dog visit.

A dog that is not given treats by people on therapy dog visits will be less distracted by food encountered on a visit, since it won't be expecting any. When a dog is expecting to eat, it may drool. On a therapy dog visit, drooling is a nuisance.

Another potential accident possibility is when a disoriented person grabs the dog and doesn't let go. The person may grab feet, ears, tail or the whole dog. Of course, if you see that this might happen, the best thing to do is to keep the dog out of that person's reach. You simply aren't helping people when you let them abuse a dog, even if they don't know what they're doing. Besides hurting the dog and possibly ruining it as a therapy dog, such incidents may make other people in the facility dislike that person. Such people (and your dog) must be protected from their own erratic behavior.

When the worst happens and you find yourself dealing with a dog being clutched by someone, your first concern must be to keep the dog calm. Get the dog focused on your voice. Hold the dog steady if you can get your hands in. You may want to encircle the dog's muzzle with one hand. Scratch the dog behind the ears as you would during an injection, to distract its pain senses. Massaging a muscle with your hand may also help. Avoid shouting or making any sudden movement that might trigger your dog to try and protect itself or you. If you must call for help, keep panic out of your voice. Lift your chin and project your voice so it will carry, but don't let it convey fear to your dog.

If you can get staff help, let the staff member pry the person's hands away, while you give your full support to the dog. If you don't have help, try to hold the dog's focus with your voice while you steadily pry the clutching hands away.

With experience, you will be able to avoid almost all such incidents, which is why a therapy dog working with an experienced handler feels far less stress than with a beginning handler.

In the unlikely event of a therapy dog biting someone, the law must be followed. It varies from state to state, but in general the bite is to be reported to authorities, first aid and any further medical attention given, and the handler must assume responsibility. Rendering aid immediately and showing sincere concern often reduces the risk of a lawsuit later. Always carry identification and proof of a veterinarian-administered rabies vaccination when working a dog in public. You may have to surrender your dog for quarantine at a shelter or veterinary hospital, at your expense.

In the event of a bite to the top of the shoulders, neck or head, the situation could become tragic. Health officials might judge it unwise to risk that the dog's vaccination could have failed. A bite near the brain is thought to be able to transmit rabies before results of quarantining the dog would be known. In some places, your vacci-

Similar to the hold put on a therapy dog during vet visits, it is advisable to handle a dog as shown here to prepare it for the possibility of being in the grip of an Alzheimer's patient or other person who doesn't understand the dog is being made uncomfortable. The need to proof a dog against retaliating during such incidents is obvious in therapy applications.

nated therapy dog might be ordered destroyed for testing. Let's hope science will give us an alternative.

After a dog bite, the handler, any group he or she represents and the facility could be liable to lawsuit. Several factors would make you more likely to be sued or to lose a lawsuit. If the dog has had any training to bite humans, has known aggressive tendencies, was out of control at the time or lacks training, your liability could be increased. Owners of large dogs, especially breeds perceived as aggressive, are more vulnerable to lawsuit. People are incredibly forgiving in everyday life when small dogs bite humans, which is probably why small dogs do a lot more biting than do large dogs.

It's obvious that you don't want your therapy dog to bite anyone. The best protection against such a terrible experience is your constant attention to the dog on therapy dog visits. Be aware that the most likely cause of a dog bite would be if someone hurt or terrified the dog and it felt cornered and unprotected. Be there for your dog. Dog bites from therapy dogs are extremely rare, and good handlers will keep it that way.

Handler attention is also a major consideration in whether or not you should take more than one dog on a therapy dog visit. In general, the rule is no more than one dog per handler. It's difficult to give your attention to more than one dog working at once—and unlikely that you'll consistently be able to do so.

There are a few exceptions to this rule. If you train your dogs to be handled by others, a staff person or someone else in the facility might handle an extra dog you bring on a therapy dog visit. That would leave it to you to supervise. You might also bring an extra volunteer who doesn't have a therapy dog—or whose dog is out of service for some reason—to handle one of your dogs.

There are cases where dogs work closely as a team for one handler, so that one handler could control and protect multiple dogs on a therapy dog visit. This would be a matter of special training and an exceptional handler.

9.8. TERRITORIAL RANGES, POSITIONS

Another aspect of the handler's job is understanding territorial ranges and using them to advantage. People have territorial ranges for various situations, and so do dogs.

Fearful People

Your work with your dog in public on social skills should prepare you to "read" people's faces and decide whether or not they feel at ease with your dog. If you see that they don't—or if some comment indicates this to you—you can learn through experience and by watching people's faces and body language how far you need to stay back with the dog to avoid making them uncomfortable. Six feet is enough for some, twenty feet or more for others.

At the right distance, the person can see your body language and the dog's, but doesn't feel threatened. At this range you can use positions in place. Perhaps later the person will feel like petting the dog, but never push.

You can also move outside the territorial range to interact with other people with the dog, and see if this puts the fearful person at ease. Some people aren't actually afraid, just somewhat "goosey." It can be part of a medical problem, or even behavior the person has developed to get attention. With experience you'll learn to recognize this.

Regardless of their reasons, people should never have a dog forced on them. Consider the territorial range as space to which they're entitled.

Giving the Dog Room to Move Away

Saint taught me something about the dog's territorial range. One day we visited a preschool for children with disabilities. A tiny boy crawled around fast, drooling profusely. At first, he and Saint mutually enjoyed having Saint wash his face. But when the child crawled at Saint and backed the dog up about twenty feet, Saint decided to stop him.

Saint didn't bite or snap. Instead, he said something to the child in a fraction of a second using unmistakable language. The child was stunned. The teacher told the child how far faces need to be apart. (I gathered that this child did the same with people.) I took

Saint's muzzle instantly and spoke to him quietly, my nose to his, to remind him it's not his job to correct children.

This is an example of how the handler must protect the dog so the dog won't decide to take responsibility for the situation. Saint treated the child as he would treat a puppy, and he is extremely gentle with puppies and small dogs as well as children. He would not have hurt the child, except by accident. Since he is so accustomed to having people in his face, an accidental injury would have been unlikely. Being well prepared allowed us to survive my handler error. I should never have allowed Saint to be backed up like that for such a distance.

This experience, as well as some others with people crowding my dogs, taught me not to corner the dog. The therapy dog needs room to move away if someone puts too much pressure on it. The handler isn't always sure exactly how much pressure the dog is feeling.

Protecting the dog's territorial range means watching out for the following:

1. Don't block the dog with your body or the leash. If you need to physically position the dog, get the dog set and then take the pressure off. Be ready to move back if the dog wants to move away from a person.
2. Don't let a crowd surround your dog. When working a therapy dog in a large group of people, stay on your feet and circulate, dealing with a few people at a time.
3. Don't get backed up against a wall, where you and the dog have no escape from a press of people.
4. Your dog may enjoy having several people pet it at once, but be especially alert at such times. It's easy to overlook the one hand that may inflict pain on the dog. Avoid having too many small children petting the dog at one time. Three or four is about right with children under age seven. They aren't always gentle, and their faces are right in the dog's face.
5. Don't let people keep coming at the dog and backing the dog up. Get staff help to interrupt this if necessary.

Other helpful aspects regarding "territory" deal with ways to use space and to position your dog to more effectively help people.

Therapy dogs elicit different responses at different levels. A small dog on a chair or low table may stimulate a person's interest more than if it were on the floor.

Putting Yourself on the Other Person's Level

When practical, put yourself on the same level as the people to whom you're talking. Sometimes I get a footstool or lightweight chair to move around with me, or a seat next to the person or small group the dog and I are working with. It makes seated people more comfortable—not having to bend their necks to look up at me—and lets them know I'm willing to take unhurried time with them. It also makes the visit less tiring for me. Since you need to spend about fifteen minutes or longer with a person in order to do a good visit in many cases, sitting is sensible.

Using the Dog's Position to Reach People

I've noticed that putting the dog in different positions often gets more response from people. Some people respond strongly to a dog placed on their laps, although you must do this with caution. Instead, you can sit near people and hold the dog on your lap so they can reach it. This has a completely different effect than that of a dog on the floor. I've also seen great responses from people when a dog is placed on furniture near them. This can be a chair next to a person in a wheelchair, a person's bed, a sofa next to a person or other arrangement.

When the furniture is plastic coated, I sometimes put the dog right on it, and just brush the dog hair off afterward. Otherwise, I put a towel on the furniture under the dog. The towel catches hair that could otherwise get onto people's clothing later, and eliminates complaints about the dog being on furniture. Towels come in sizes to accommodate even the largest dogs.

Another way to position the dog is to have it lie on its back. Angel likes to loll in my arms on her back. This appeals to people—and well it might, because a dog in this position demonstrates submissiveness and total trust. It puts people at ease with the dog. Dogs too large to hold this way may lie on their backs on the floor for petting. This also touches a chord in people. Be sure to protect your dog when lying on its back, because mistreatment in such an ultra-submissive position on the floor could destroy the dog's trust. Never force a dog to take this position on a therapy dog visit—it must be the dog's choice.

Even large dogs can join people on the couch during a therapy visit. In this position, the dog may seem less threatening to the person it is with.

When a dog willingly lies on its back in a person's arm or on the floor, it is a signal of the dog's complete trust. If your therapy dog does this at home, never insist that it do so on therapy visits. If it takes the position on its own, be sure that no one has a chance to injure or mistreat it—even without meaning to.

Working the Dog to Attract and Direct People's Attention

The handler needs to know how the dog's presence affects people with regard to a few other factors when doing visits in a facility.

1. When a dog walks in, all eyes will turn to it. If another program is in progress, keep the dog around the corner or otherwise out of sight until the program is finished. The dog walking in would seriously disrupt the other program.

2. When people need to move toward the dining room or elsewhere for specific care, you can help the staff by heading that way with the dog (up to the acceptable boundary—probably not into the dining room when food is being served) to get people to follow.

3. During some procedures, such as psychological testing for children, the dog's presence could be a severe distraction. One way to handle this is to have the dog do a quiet Down-Stay behind some sort of screen. I've used an upended mini-trampoline to good effect, or a large filing cabinet. It helps if the handler can see both the dog and the activity in the area. If the dog isn't reliable off leash, hook the leash around an immovable object. Use an area through which no one will need to pass. If your dog won't remain completely quiet, take it out of earshot.

4. It may not be a good idea to have your dog bark on command in a facility. Many people find a dog's bark frightening—even if they asked you to have the dog do it. Some people in the room may have limitations of vision or understanding. I remember one visit when I asked Angel to bark on command several times and noticed that people did not want to pet her as much that day. I've seen little children burst into tears and elderly people get terrified looks on their faces and then need much reassurance—reassurance that you can't be sure they fully understand.

   Some dogs consider barking, even on command, somewhat aggressive. When you encourage the dog to bark around people, you may encourage it to take the wrong attitude toward those people. However, some dogs, like Angel, bark from excitement rather than aggression and will not find this confusing. Barking also makes noise that may be unwelcome in a facility. Use barking cautiously, if at all. Move the dog well back from people before cuing it to bark. Be prepared to reassure people that you told the dog to do that.

There will be times during therapy visits that your activities will be put on hold and your dog must be held in some out-of-the-way location. If your therapy dog is not completely secure off-lead, find somewhere to loop a lead as shown and keep the dog in the area as directed by the facility staff.

Providing a Platform for Small Dogs

One technique I find invaluable when working my small dog is to use a platform. You can design your own, depending on your dog and the materials available to you. I use a Vari-Kennel, which is a high-quality vinyl pet carrier. I strap it to a dolly made to fit that has swivel wheels. I secure the crate to the dolly with an elastic luggage strap. With a second strap I attach towels to the back of the crate, and carry Angel's other gear inside the crate. The Vari-Kennel has a knobby surface that gives Angel good footing. It puts her at a comfortable height for people in wheelchairs or standing to pet her. Angel will do a flawless Wait on this platform—if your dog will not, you need to work differently.

The popular image of small therapy dogs is sitting on laps. In reality, most people can't hold a dog on their laps. Some are too frail, some sit with laps steeply inclined so the dog can't balance there and some clutch roughly at the dog when it's seated on them. With Angel on her platform, she's easy to reach, the person isn't bearing her weight and she's spared the risk of being held or dropped. When it's appropriate for her to sit on a lap, I offer to spread a towel there first (if the person's clothing is thin, I insist on the towel for padding), and I do the lifting. Sometimes she can step across from the platform, when I give her the word.

Angel stays much cooler working from her platform than she did when I held her over people for them to pet her. She doesn't get tired on visits anymore. This is partly because she no longer has to dodge people's feet—on her platform, no one can trip over her and this is a safety benefit for people, too. I find that Angel can interact with people more expressively from the platform than she could when held for petting. It's an effective way for a small dog to work.

I let Angel jump up onto the platform, but I lift her down. This spares her joints the impact of the jump, and encourages her to think of getting down as something I control, not to be done on her own.

Orienting the Dog to the Area

If your therapy dog is a beginner, you may find it gets overexcited and silly when you first arrive at a facility. The cure for this is a brief session of control exercises before going in.

Saint needed this for a few months; in time you will find that

Using the top of a small dog's crate as a platform offers some definite advantages during a therapy dog visit. From the vantage point of its own crate, the dog will be more confident with its visitors and they will be better able to pet the dog either sitting or standing.

Those who position their small therapy dogs on crate tops during therapy dog visits generally find that their dogs get through the visits more easily and are less tired after the visit is over.

the dog settles down without it. The routine I used was Heel first, working the dog at my side, followed by Come, working the dog at a distance. A sidewalk, parking lot or quiet hallway will all work nicely for this short drill. It should be upbeat, fast to center the dog's attention and just long enough to get the dog into gear without tiring it.

Another common problem is the dog breaking off its work to go sniff corners. This is easy to solve if you look at it from the dog's point of view. Give the dog a quick tour when you first enter the room. It saves time and the dog will work much better for you. You'll learn to do this efficiently, and people will easily understand your explanation that the dog needs to get its bearings. Humans have the same need, but we can satisfy it by looking around a room, while most dogs use their noses more than their eyes.

9.9. HANDLER AS INTERPRETER

One of the hats I wear as a therapy dog handler is that of "interpreter." I interpret the dog's behavior for people, and I interpret the situation for the dog and direct it to do the right thing. It amazes me what interpretations people will make based on a dog's behavior. I've had people think the dog wanted to bite them because it licked, sniffed or looked at them. After I explain what the dog's behavior means, these people are often instantly at ease.

Some dog behavior should be prohibited on visits, some should be interpreted for people and some should be limited and explained.

If your dog starts to bathe its posterior with its tongue, get it to stop. Distracting the dog usually works. Scratching doesn't look good, and it's not good for your dog's skin. This is not behavior you should allow your dog to do in public, nor is mounting another dog or a person. If your dog will need to relieve itself on a therapy dog visit, take it to an appropriate place beforehand. For any necessary breaks, allow it to relieve itself only in that place. Outings when you practice social skills are the time to develop your dog's control and understanding about this. Be ready to clean up after your dog in a facility in case of an accident, but with a properly trained dog you may never have to clean up except outdoors.

Licking people can give therapeutic benefits, and some people enjoy it. As interpreter, let people know that licking is a sign of affection and often of submission. Don't let the dog lick people right on the mouth, as there can be a slight risk of transmitting disease. On the first sign of someone not wanting to be licked, gently pull the dog back.

Sniffing is behavior that calls for varied handling. Of course the dog should never be allowed to sniff people's crotches. However, since sniffing is natural dog behavior used in social interaction, sometimes it's appropriate to allow the dog to sniff politely as part of a greeting. As interpreter, explain why dogs do this: dogs get the information that people get with their eyes by sniffing. In fact, dogs probably get more information, and often this information helps them relate effectively to people. If people are comfortable with the sniffing, it can even make them feel singled out for special attention.

Saint, a retired tracking dog, sniffs people's knees, then offers his head for petting. He doesn't seem to have an opinion about the scent, just a need to check it. In most situations, I think it's better to interpret for him than to alter this natural behavior that people so easily accept. Note, though, that it's part of a greeting. If the person isn't being greeted by Saint, they won't get sniffed, either. The dog should not be touching anyone unless the person wishes, and that includes sniffing.

Interpreting for a dog may be more natural to you than you realize. People often "talk for" dogs. Two people will speak back and forth, for the dog. This isn't silly. It's an attempt to verbalize a dog's nonverbal language. When at the veterinarian's office, on a therapy dog visit or elsewhere with a dog, I find this happens a lot. Other people often initiate it, including the veterinarian. It helps humans to better understand a dog's behavior, feelings and point of view.

9.10 THE HANDLER IS RESPONSIBLE

Can you sign the following statement for a facility where you want to bring your dog to visit?

1. When my dog comes to visit, its coat will be clean and free of tangles.
2. When my dog comes to visit, it will be (a) in good health; (b) free of internal parasites (hookworms, heartworms, coccidiosis, etc.); (c) free of external parasites (fleas, ticks, etc.).

It is not unusual for the therapy dog handler to have to interpret the dog's actions for people in facilities. A perceptive handler will know how to communicate and set aside natural fears so useful visits are achieved.

The degree of a therapy dog's effectiveness in relating to people is a reflection of training and conditioning. It all comes back to the handler's ability to get the dog to learn the job well and do it consistently.

210

3. My dog will have received all vaccinations, including a rabies vaccination given by a veterinarian. If the dog's vaccinations were not up to date when this series was given, the dog will not visit until two weeks after completing the series of vaccinations or the time the veterinarian feels immunization is complete.

4. My dog will be kept under control at all times. The dog will not be permitted to display or act out any aggression toward another animal or person. Some animals cannot be adequately controlled to protect others—I WILL NOT BRING SUCH A DOG INTO THIS FACILITY. I will get whatever training I need to be able to completely control my dog. I will make sure the dog is adequately socialized to people and to other animals before visiting this facility. I understand that an animal can cause serious injury, especially to vulnerable people, by tripping or scratching them as well as by biting, and I will control my dog to prevent such injuries. I will also protect my dog at all times from any and all abuse, as an abused dog can become dangerous.

5. My dog is housebroken. If there is an accident, I will clean it up. I will take my dog to whatever area the facility designates for dogs to relieve themselves, and I will pick up after my dog in this area also.

6. I have insurance that covers liability if my dog injures anyone.

Signature: _____

Such a statement would be a good idea for facilities to use for dogs that are brought in, and to make sure owners are aware of their responsibilities. As facilities and therapy dog organizations consider rules and qualifications, the handler must always be the key. No dog should work without a handler. With this dependable person on the scene, who is responsible by law for the dog's behavior, all is well.

Therapy dog work happens on the local, personal level. The public recognizes reliable handlers, while the staff of every facility eliminates handlers and dogs they don't completely trust. No matter what certifications they have, poor handlers will not be invited back. Facilities must always have this freedom, and it's the handler's job to earn their trust.

This book is not intended to frighten people about the risks of therapy dog work. That would be silly, because the risks are extremely low. When it comes to therapy dog work, the sky is not falling. Instead, the purpose of this book is to help handlers learn to control and protect their dogs and to put people at ease with skill and courtesy. The best way to protect people and dogs in therapy dog work is to provide each dog with a good handler.

Therapy dog work isn't so mysterious. We have the knowledge to take care of the dogs, to condition them to handling, to train them for control, to teach them social skills and to handle them responsibly with people. A trained therapy dog is a joy to live and work with. A good therapy dog handler is an asset to the community. If you are blessed with the opportunity to do this job, I hope you will find it, as I have, the most fulfilling thing you'll ever do with your dog.